THE POWER OF FAITH

THE POWER OF FAITH

A JOURNEY TO HEALING, WHOLENESS, AND HARMONY

ARIEL PAZ

iUniverse LLC
Bloomington

THE POWER OF FAITH
A journey to healing, wholeness, and harmony

iUniverse books may be ordered through booksellers or by contacting:

iUniverse LLC
1663 Liberty Drive
Bloomington, IN 47403
www.iuniverse.com
1-800-Authors (1-800-288-4677)

ISBN: 978-1-4620-5743-6 (sc)
ISBN: 978-1-4620-5745-0 (hc)
ISBN: 978-1-4620-5744-3 (e)

Printed in the United States of America

iUniverse rev. date: 01/24/2014

CONTENTS

Acknowledgments vii
Introduction ix

The Phases of Faith

Phase 1: Preparation

Chapter 1: How Did I Get Here? 1
Chapter 2: Make Mistakes 14
Chapter 3: Experience Trials 22
Chapter 4: Choose to Surrender 29

Phase 2: Practice

Chapter 5: Focus on God's Strength 38
Chapter 6: Learn to Be Responsible 48
Chapter 7: Let Your Life Be Transformed 61
Chapter 8: Learn to Wait 67
Chapter 9: Learn to Be Humble 72
Chapter 10: God Is on Your Side 85
Chapter 11: Face Your Fears 93
Chapter 12: Learn to Listen 105
Chapter 13: Keep the Faith 119

Phase 3: Purpose

Chapter 14: God Has the Plan 135
Chapter 15: Be Set Free 141
Chapter 16: Lighten Up 149
Chapter 17: Live in Harmony 159

Prayers for Meditation and Recitation 165

Appendices

Appendix A: Translations 169
Appendix B: Bibliography and Works Cited 171

Author Bio 173

Dedication

I would like to dedicate this book to my two sons who have taught me so much about love, forgiveness, and acceptance. Thank you for being who you are from the bottom of my heart.

ACKNOWLEDGMENTS

Heartfelt thanks to all my friends and loved ones who supported and assisted me in my journey to faith, healing, and in the writing and publication of this book.

Thank you to my dear friends, Mimi and Kim, for your support, encouragement, feedback and editing assistance. I am so grateful to have you in my life.

To my youngest son for your words of wisdom, insight, and your humorous way of making me laugh. I love you so much.

The greatest thank you of all to my Lord and Savior, Jesus Christ, whose grace, mercy, forgiveness and love are unfathomable.

INTRODUCTION

Hurt, heartache, and disappointment are inevitable in life. Difficult experiences cause us to lose the innate trust we were born with. The good news is we don't have to remain the walking wounded. Healing and wholeness are possible. We can unleash the flow of blessings into our lives by activating the secret power each of us possess.

Some call it believing. I call it Faith.

Faith is a seed that lies deep within us. When watered and nurtured, this seed will grow into a huge tree that will bear much fruit in our lives and in the lives of others. Once firmly rooted, Faith is the foundation that keeps us grounded during the hurricanes of life.

I like to think of Faith as a spiritual muscle we all possess. In the same way exercise strengthens our physical muscles, exercising our faith strengthens our spiritual muscle. The more we use it, the more it grows. Faith is believing in a better tomorrow and a brighter future, even when things seem hopeless and the pain of yesterday is almost too much to bear. It is the fuel that fires up our engine to move forward. What's more exciting is Faith opens the channel for great blessings to flow into our lives.

We all endure difficult circumstances, but we have a choice in how to respond. When we learn to view our situations through the eyes of Faith instead of fear, and realize trials are meant to strengthen and transform us, we activate an unseen force. This power works on our behalf to bring the body, mind, and spirit into wholeness, to heal the broken parts, and to restore harmony in our lives. The harp on the front cover symbolizes healing from emotional and physical wounds and also communication with the divine. It represents beautifully the message I wish to share; we all have been wounded in some way and we all possess the power to be healed.

Whatever your belief system, you can activate this amazing gift. You, too, can be healed from your past, transform your future, and experience more peace, power, and joy than ever before.

There comes a crossroad in our lives when our eyes are opened and we see the world from a different perspective. I believe this book will be that crossroad in your life. If you are willing, take the first step and embark upon an exciting journey that will last your entire lifetime. You have nothing to lose and everything to gain.

And now, here's my story.

CHAPTER 1

How Did I Get Here?

"I can't take it anymore, God," I cried out as I fell to my knees on my kitchen floor, helpless against the realization that there was nothing else I could do to save my marriage. My body writhed in protest against the finality of it all, and thoughts of suicide drifted in and out of my mind.

I feel like I'm dead, yet I'm still alive. This is what it must feel like to be crucified.

I knew I was in trouble and needed help. Sobbing and desperate, I crawled toward the wall where the phone hung. I reached for the phone and dialed my counselor's number.

"I'm having suicidal thoughts," I said in a voice devoid of emotion.

"You need to come in right away," she replied.

Hours later, I slumped in the Queen Anne-style chair in her office, motionless and confused.

"I can't quite describe what's going on. It's like my mind is clouded and fuzzy. All I know is that when I had these thoughts of killing myself, I knew I had to call you."

"You're depressed," she said. "You need to start on some medication."

"I feel like I am losing my mind," I whimpered.

The foundation of my life had crumbled. My boss had asked me take time off work. I later found out it was because a friend had told him how emotional I had been at the office. I couldn't keep up with my night-school work, and my children had gone to stay with their grandparents, as I was in no condition to care for them.

Everything was collapsing all around me, and I was losing control.

How on earth did I get here?

"Start from the beginning," the counselor suggested, and so I did.

The Early Years

Born in the late 1950s, I was the first of two daughters. My father, Armando, was the suave, Casanova-type, with a heavy Spanish accent. His father was from Spain and worked as a dealer in a casino in Florida. Dad learned at an early age to smoke, drink, and manipulate a deck of cards. My mother, Maria, on the other hand, was a young, naïve Greek girl. Her father had been a candymaker, who died when she was only six years old. As the baby in the family, Maria's brothers and sisters always told her what to do. As a result, she grew up not having much need or opportunity to think for herself or make decisions on her own.

My parents met in New Orleans, at a restaurant where Dad was working as a waiter at the time. Mom worked for the airlines and had flown in for the weekend with her girlfriend. Dad's Spanish accent, dark good looks, and smooth demeanor swept Mom off her feet, and a tumultuous and torrid love affair soon began.

Within a few months, my father moved to the East Coast to be with the woman he loved and got a job at a well-known restaurant in the city.

Despite her family's objections and disapproval, Mom followed her heart and married her sweetheart. The couple bought a general store and worked long hours, seven days a week, for the next three and a half years.

"I need a fresh start," Armando announced one day. Meanwhile, Maria was expecting their first child.

A month after I was born, the couple moved across the country to settle in Las Vegas, Nevada. Dad dreamed of working in a casino, as his father had. Leaving her family and friends behind, my mother moved to a new and exciting city on the other side of the country.

Unfortunately, the penniless couple was unable to pay the dues required to join the union, so Dad was unable to get a job in any casino. Mom was forced to find a job, leaving Dad at home to care for the newborn baby.

The "fresh start" didn't last long. Only a year and a half later, the couple moved again—this time to Hollywood. Mom was tired, overworked, and expecting her second child when she discovered a terrible secret.

Telltale lipstick-stained cigarette stubs in the family car were a sickening clue.

Dad was having an affair with another woman.

"How could you do this to me when I'm pregnant with your child?" Maria screamed.

Furious, heartbroken, and disillusioned, she packed up her belongings and her baby and moved out. Despite her anger, the reality of having a second child, living in a strange state, and having no one to turn to set in.

"Please let me come back. I promise I'll change," Dad swore.

Mom relented and decided to give Dad another chance. My sister, Eleni, was born in August of that year. The couple now had two small children to care for.

Actions speak louder than words.
Be sure to see real change before believing someone's pretty promises.

Childhood Memories

"Tell me what you remember about your childhood," my counselor prompted.

The mind has a convenient way of forgetting the painful events of our past. Most of my childhood memories have long since faded deep into my subconscious, and bringing them up is as arduous as digging up a grave.

There were some happy memories. It was Christmas, and I was about six or seven years old. "Look under the tree," Daddy said. There was a dollhouse—the most exquisite dollhouse I had ever seen. It had all sorts of tiny furniture and even a miniature family with kids. Daddy had put it together the night before.

"I love it, Daddy," I squealed. The dollhouse was a treasured toy for many, many years. Perhaps, in some magical way, the miniature toy family symbolized the dream of a perfect family a small girl wished was hers.

I also remember Daddy holding the seat of my bike in my first attempts at riding a two-wheeler, Mom teaching me how to swim while we were on vacation at the beach, and learning how to skate at the local ice rink. These few precious times stand out like jewels, shining among the dark clouds of hurtful times and things long forgotten.

Then there were the painful memories.

Unhappy Memories

As a protective measure, the conscious mind remembers only snippets of visions: Dad sleeping off his liquor on the sofa, the yelling and screaming, furniture thrown out the window in the middle of a fight. There was a gun in the house, and when the fighting would begin, one of my parents would inevitably retrieve it and brandish it about. Eleni and I were terrified, and the neighbors often called the police. Ours was not a peaceful home, but unfortunately, it was all I knew. Dysfunction became the norm, and I never knew what it was like to have a loving, caring, or emotionally available father.

"I'm going to make myself a martini," Dad would say, the smell of alcohol still on his breath from the night before.

"But it's only ten o'clock in the morning," Mom would reply, her voice tremulous.

"So what?" he would ask, thinking nothing of it. We all knew the pattern, and with each drink, the tension mounted in the family. Neither parent could see the signs of a drinking problem, or perhaps they were both in denial.

Early and frequent use of alcohol is a sign of abuse. Be aware.

Although he had a brilliant mind for business, Dad could not keep off the booze, which caused him to lose one job after another.

"I need a fresh start," Dad would say whenever he lost his job.

"Did you get fired again?" Mom asked, the same old tune repeating itself like a broken record. It was a never-ending cycle.

"Are we going to have money to pay the rent, Mom?"

Worries about whether my parents would have enough money to pay the bills and the rent, and when the electricity would be cut off next, became familiar friends of mine. At a tender age, I felt responsible for things over which I had no control. Instead of the carefree mind of a child, worry and anxiousness became my normal state of mind.

Years later, Mom and I tallied up the number of times we moved while I was growing up—a grand total of thirty-one times, and this only counted the ones she could remember. It was like being in the military, except Dad could never keep a job.

As a shy child, entering new schools and neighborhoods every few years was quite a challenge. Eventually, I overcame my shyness and learned to make friends quickly, but all the moving took its toll on me. I developed a strong aversion to relocating that would plague me into adulthood.

Painful emotional experiences from the past will continue to haunt us until we face and deal with them.

A Critical Home

In addition to developing an anxious spirit and an aversion to moving, I also became desensitized to my own feelings and emotions. My mother constantly told me that I was "overly sensitive," and I came to believe this was true. She often related the story of how when I was a little girl, I was so upset the first time I saw my shadow I didn't want to step on it. Another time when we were at the market, I cried when I saw the dead chickens in the meat department case.

These comments instilled in me a sense of shame and an unconscious decision to bury my feelings. I learned the lie that feelings were bad and that something was wrong with me because I had them.

"I have to say that I love my mother very much, and we are very close. She did the best she could raising us," I said to the counselor.

"I understand. Go on," the counselor replied.

"My mother was very critical of me. I strove to excel at school so that she would be proud of me. I remember one day bringing home my report card: all As and a B in English."

"What happened in English?" was her first comment. Wow. That stung.

So, I learned that I needed to be perfect to be accepted by both my parents, particularly by my mother. I tried to excel at everything I did to the extent that I would stress myself out and get migraine headaches. That was the result of these patterns of thinking I learned early in life.

Critical parents produce children who don't feel approved or accepted.

Eroding Faith

The first experience with faith and trust most people have is with their family of origin. Unfortunately, Dad was never there for us emotionally or physically, but it wasn't until adulthood that I would face the deep sadness of this loss. Dad's promises of a new and better life never materialized due to his drinking problem. Repeated broken promises and disappointments were too much to handle as a small child, so I learned to suppress and ignore these feelings as well to avoid the pain. I also learned not to trust, believe, or have faith in my father.

Factors such as having an abusive, absent, or emotionally detached parent can distort our perception of a good and loving God. Although we may not consciously be aware that this is what has happened, coming to grips with the reality of our losses and hurts helps us to move forward on our spiritual path. How we related to our parents also affects our relationship with God. The loss of a parent while young can also impact our view of a Heavenly Father.

How we view our parents impacts how we view God.

When I was about nine or ten years old, Dad, being the brilliant entrepreneur that he was, had a great idea. Mom had recently returned from a trip to Greece with her mother and shared with Dad the lack of American products and services in Greece at the time.

"They don't even have a McDonald's," Mom said.

That was the spark.

Dad decided he wanted to open up a McDonald's-type fast-food restaurant in Athens, Greece.

"It will make a million dollars, like it did here in America," he said. This was in the 1970s, and there was nothing like that in Greece at the time. "All I need to do is find a rich businessman to back me financially." Dad was a smooth talker and had soon persuaded the owner of a famous Washingtonian steakhouse to go in on the venture and provide the financial backing needed for the endeavor. It was the opportunity of a lifetime.

Shooting for the Stars

Our family was very excited. When we arrived in Athens, we rented an apartment in Kolonaki, a ritzy part of town. It was a very nice neighborhood, with lots of shops, shoe stores, and art galleries.

"Let's go to the bakery!" Mom would announce in the morning.

In the early morning hours, Mom, Eleni, and I would walk to the local bakery to buy freshly baked bread. Holding the soft, warm bread in my arms, it was quite a temptation not to bite into it on the way back.

"Wait till we get home," Mom would say.

Enticed by the aroma of the warm bread, we hurried home, where we would slather it with butter and feta cheese, a tangy Greek cheese made of goat's milk. To this day, the smell and taste of warm bread still evokes the pleasures of those early-morning breakfasts in Greece.

Things must have been going well with the business, because one day, Dad brought home a Mercedes. It was green and had soft, beige, leather seats that made sitting in the backseat a joy. Dad had a weakness for fancy cars. He also decided to move us into a large villa in the countryside of Athens, in a section of town called Palio Psyhico. Our family had several pets: two dogs, two rabbits, and a turtle that ate bananas.

Eleni and I attended a private Catholic school that required us to wear uniforms and catch the bus at 6:30 in the morning. In the evenings, we had a Greek tutor. Mom and Dad got along better, since Dad wasn't drinking as much.

We were starting to resemble a normal family at last. It was almost time for the restaurant to open, and all was going well, until . . .

The Owner's Son

The owner's son came to Greece from America to visit the operation. He was very impressed with everything my dad had done to design the restaurant—especially since my dad didn't speak the language.

"I want to run this place when it opens," he told my father.

"After all the work I've put into this place, now you come in at the last minute and want to take all the credit?" Dad's face got beet red, and this time, it wasn't from alcohol.

The battle ensued between the owner, who backed his son, and my father, who insisted that he should be the one to open the store. As one might guess, the owner won. The money stopped, and the restaurant never opened.

It was a dismal failure for our entire family. Everyone's hopes were crushed, and we returned to the States penniless, disgraced, and discouraged.

"Be careful about shooting for the stars," Dad warned ruefully. "It's a long way to fall if you don't make it."

The Last Straw

Feeling like a failure once again, Dad went back to the comfort of his martinis. Despite all the abuse, instability, and unfaithfulness, deep down inside, my parents must have really loved each other. Perhaps that is what made it so hard for Mom to leave and for Dad to stay away for very long. They didn't know how to solve their problems. In those days, these kinds of issues were taboo and rarely discussed in public.

As Eleni and I got older, we realized how bad things were and knew we would all be better off without our drunken, irresponsible, philandering father. "At least we will have peace," we pleaded to our mother.

Setting boundaries in our relationships protects us from being repeatedly hurt and abused.

Mom had taken Dad back umpteen times—always trusting, always forgiving, always hoping—but never setting any boundaries or demanding changes in his behavior before taking him back. Each time she took him in, he reverted to his old self and his drinking.

"You'll never change, Armando," Mom repeated with sad resignation.

"I promise I'll give you a better life," Dad cajoled. "Move with me to Florida, and I'll prove it to you."

One more time, Mom agreed to give him another chance.

One more time, we summoned up hope, packed our things, and moved.

In Florida, we were captives in the duplex he had rented. With no car to go anywhere, we had no freedom at all.

"It's like we're in prison here. I've had enough," Mom announced one day, with a tone of finality in her voice we had never before heard.

Change occurs when the pain of staying the same outweighs the pain of changing.

Combing the newspapers, Mom found someone looking to share the expenses of a drive back east. One day while Dad was away, she packed our few belongings. The stranger who answered our prayers picked us up, and we headed back home, like refugees in the back of his van.

The End of a Marriage

It took quite a few years for Dad to realize he had lost his family for good. Somehow, he would keep track of where we were living and unexpectedly show up at the door of our apartment to see if Mom would take him back. His loud pounding on the door terrified us, and Mom would threaten to call the police in order to get him to leave. Although the drama continued in our lives, Eleni and I were thankful that Mom had finally mustered the courage to stand up to Dad.

The visits got fewer and fewer, but Dad would still pop in and out of our lives over the next several years with a card or a phone call. His words were temptingly sweet, and each time, Mom would agonize over how to handle the communication.

Stand firm against the manipulative tactics of addicts.

We eventually realized that Dad would contact us for one of two reasons: either he was desperate for money or he needed a place to stay. His irresponsible lifestyle continued to plague our family.

Dad also never accepted any responsibility for the divorce. He would blame Mom for all their problems, accusing her of having an affair with her boss or some other guy at her office. All the while, he was the one having the affairs. It was a classic case of projection: he was projecting onto her the guilt he carried for his transgressions, because he was unable to face his own issues.

Nor did Dad ever admit he had a drinking problem. Who knows what caused him to drink so heavily? Perhaps it was his insecurities and fears. Rather than deal with the hurt and pain he felt, he turned to alcohol for comfort.

Many of us do the same thing. We develop destructive and unhealthy behaviors, such as drinking or drug abuse, overeating, overworking, or overachieving, to numb our feelings and emotions. Little do we realize the pain never goes away, until we face the root of the problem and deal with it in a healthy manner.

Unhealthy, destructive, and excessive behaviors are a sign of unresolved emotional pain. Once we uncover the root cause of our pain, we can begin to heal by replacing these behaviors with healthy ones.

Settling Down

Now that Dad was out of the picture, it was time for the three of us to start a new life. We settled back in the suburbs of Baltimore, and Eleni and I enrolled in yet another new school. But this time was different. It was time to begin establishing roots. Eager to make friends, I became involved in a myriad of extracurricular activities. While other kids moaned and groaned about school and cut classes, I thought school was fun. The excitement of school activities replaced the excitement of a tumultuous home life.

It was also time for Mom to get back to church.

Going to Church

"We're going to church," Mom announced one day. We began attending a Greek Orthodox church not far from where we lived. Although we were not regular attendees, and Eleni and I never went to Sunday school, the Greek church was my first exposure to anything of a religious nature.

Ritual and tradition were a big part of the church we attended. The choir would sing and much of the service was in Greek, although many of the congregation, including Eleni and I, didn't understand a word. Whenever we dared ask Mom what was being said, all she would say was, "Shhhh! No talking in church."

The priest would pray in Greek, while swinging some kind of contraption that sprinkled incense all over the place. Then, he would disappear behind the closed doors of the altar.

Wonder what he is doing back there behind those closed doors?

Meanwhile, the psalmists, or "psalti" as they are called, moaned in odd-pitched tones. The congregation would stand and sit, stand and sit, stand and sit, and Mom would admonish us to, "Do your cross," which we had to do three times about a million times in any given service. I found church boring and repetitive, and if God was there, I never knew Him.

When religious ritual loses its meaning, we lose connection to God.

An Introduction to God

As high school graduation neared, Mom and I both worked hard, applying for scholarships for me to go to college. Good grades and a low family income resulted in two scholarships, which would completely pay for four years of college tuition. It was an opportunity for a better life than Mom had, and I was very thankful.

"Why don't you go to the college your uncle went to? He's a lawyer now, you know," Mom suggested.

Ma wanted me to go to a school about twenty minutes from home. Like many college-bound students, I wanted to go out of state. The college I dreamed of attending was the University of Southern California, but the futility of that dream soon became apparent, and I agreed to go in state.

Foreign languages had always come easily in school, so I decided to major in French and Spanish. Having some command of the Greek language as well, my dream was to move to New York City, become an interpreter, and work for the United Nations. Sadly, this dream never materialized due to the choices I would soon make.

The college required all students to take a theology course. My professor was a Jesuit priest, who was extremely knowledgeable about the Bible. He had us read a book that explained how the Bible had been compiled from many different manuscripts that were discovered over the centuries. The course was fascinating and kindled a desire in me to read the Bible from cover to cover. At that time in my life, it was like reading a novel: some parts were interesting and some boring.

Little did I know then, but that course was my introduction to God and created a hunger to learn more about this unfamiliar God of the universe who had created me. It was just in time, because I was about to make a big mistake.

Step to Faith: Have an open mind and heart.

When we are ready to meet God, He is ready to meet us.

CHAPTER 2

Make Mistakes

Have you ever made a decision that turned out to be a big mistake? Almost everyone has at some time or another. Something doesn't feel quite right for whatever reason, but we decide to go ahead with our decision anyway. It might have been a career choice or perhaps a business or financial decision that went awry. Perhaps it was a relationship decision.

Do not despair. Good things can come out of even the worst circumstances.

Early Dating

I didn't date very much growing up. Shy, studious, and a bit on the heavy side, you could say I was a homebody of sorts. I enjoyed practicing my violin, doing needlecraft, and reading. In high school, though, I began to come out of my cocoon and started to notice boys.

The love of my life in high school was a tall Italian guy named Robert. He was muscular, quiet, and very smart. His sister and I were good friends, and she despised the girl he was dating at the time.

"I wish my brother would ask you out. You two would make a cute couple," she'd say in home economics class, as we sat together working on our projects.

Rob was in a couple of my classes and began sitting with me at study hall, much to my surprise.

One day, he leaned very close and whispered, "Would you like to go to the prom with me?" I couldn't believe it. My dream had come true. I had a date to the senior prom with the smartest and most handsome guy I knew. I was floating on air.

Mom and I were so excited preparing for the big occasion. I had chosen a beautiful, rose-colored, organza gown, trimmed with ruffles at the shoulders and the hem. A small tiara topped my chestnut curls and I felt like Scarlett O'Hara, waiting for Rhett Butler.

Rob showed up at my door. Taking a deep breath, I opened the door, and there he was, dressed in a white tux with brown trim and looking extremely dashing. He came in and handed me a small box containing a lovely corsage.

"You look so nice," I exclaimed.

"You do, too," he replied.

Off we went to his parents' house to take pictures and then on to the prom. It was a wonderful evening, and I felt like I was in heaven the entire night.

After graduating high school, Rob went off to college. We kept in touch by mail for a while, but it seemed he wasn't very interested, and we lost contact. I don't think I ever got over him.

Around this time, Mom must have decided she needed to pitch in and help me with my love life. She was always trying to match me up with somebody. Maybe it's a Greek thing, like in the movie *My Big Fat Greek Wedding.*

First, there was the heavy-set Greek guy who wore a lot of cologne. Mom was always telling me to, "Marry a Greek." He was nice enough, friendly, and outgoing, but definitely not my type. I think he really liked me, but I was, "just not that into him," as they say.

Next, there was the bearded car mechanic, the son of one of Mom's coworkers. Mom suggested he work on my car, since it was having problems at the time. We dated for six months or so. He was several years older and ready to get married. I realized I wasn't that crazy about him, so it was time to move on from that situation as well.

"Look at that good dancer over there," Mom raved one evening at a Greek festival our church put on annually. I turned to see a young man, probably in his late twenties, kicking his feet into the air, while dancing and clapping his hands to the loud Greek music.

"I wonder if he's Greek? Why don't you go over, and introduce yourself to him?" she suggested, apparently taken by his enthusiastic dancing.

"He doesn't look Greek to me," I replied nonchalantly. "Why don't *you* go over and introduce yourself?" I had recently broken up with the car mechanic and was not the least bit interested in starting a new relationship.

Before I knew it, she was out of her seat and heading toward the young Greek man.

A few minutes later, Mom came back, beaming. "His name is Stelios, and I asked him if he would teach us some of his dance steps next week."

Oh, brother, here we go again.

The following week, while I was at work at a local movie theater, Mom called me to tell me that she had invited Stelios to come over to the house a give us a Greek dance lesson before we went to the dance studio on Saturday night.

"That's fine," I said, "but I am going to the dance by myself in my own car afterward."

Saturday night arrived, and I was looking forward to going dancing, but not at all looking forward to the Greek dance lesson.

There was a knock on the door.

It was Stelios. Unexcited, I said hello and called for Mom. She, however, was very excited.

"Oh, it's so nice of you to come over and show us your dance steps. You are such a good dancer!" Mom fawned.

Oh, brother.

Wasting no time, Stelios launched into a tutorial of Greek dance steps right there in our living room, and before I knew it, it was time to leave for the studio.

"Would you like to ride with me?" Stelios asked.

"That would be fine," I said, not knowing how to decline his invitation in a polite way. This was the beginning of a pattern of not knowing how to say no to men, a symptom of people-pleasing I was to learn about years later at Al-Anon meetings.

Looks like I'm going in his car after all. Oh well, what can it hurt?

Stelios turned out to be charming, employed, financially well off, and had his own car. I even liked the cologne he wore. Quite a difference from my mostly unemployed father, who reeked of alcohol, or any of the other guys I had dated, that's for sure. In addition, he was Greek, so we had the same ethnic and religious background, and a good dancer. At eighteen, I thought that these factors were important.

When choosing a partner, look for deeper qualities such as character, commitment & communication rather than the superficial.

The Big Mistake

We started dating. Stelios would stop by the movie theater, where I worked as a cashier in the evenings, and bring me flowers for no reason. He'd call me from work to say hello, and soon, I found myself anticipating his calls with excitement. You could say I was falling for him. It wouldn't be the last time flowers and phone calls would lure me into a relationship.

One night, we were practicing dancing at his apartment. It was getting late. I don't remember exactly how it happened, but the next thing I knew, I was in his bed.

How could I have done this? I feel horrible.

Guilt and shame rushed over me like a wave in the ocean of emotions: another painful example of not being able to say no.

"Don't have sex with anyone unless you are going to marry them," my mother had warned over the years. Her words reverberated in my ears. I was very young and had hardly dated. Stelios seemed to be everything I thought I wanted at the time.

Well, now you've gone and done it. Now you have to marry this guy.

There are lots of good reasons to marry. Guilt is not one of them.

Getting Engaged

We had been dating about a year, and things were going pretty well between us. It was Valentine's Day.

"I made reservations at Tio Pepe's for Valentine's Day," Stelios said.

"Wow, that's such a nice Spanish restaurant, and I love their food," I replied in delight.

Tio Pepe's was the ultimate in class in those days. The Spanish décor and white stucco walls gave the place an authentic atmosphere, and the waiters all spoke Spanish and had a familiar accent that I loved.

We had cocktails at the bar while waiting for our table. Soon, the maître d' called our name and led us to a cozy room that we shared with a few other guests.

Stelios spared no expense and ordered a bottle of Puilly Fuisse, a fine French wine, and a pitcher of the restaurant's famous sangria. By the time we finished dinner, I was feeling very relaxed, possibly even intoxicated. The other guests had departed, and we had the room all to ourselves.

Stelios called a waiter to come in and asked him to take pictures of us with his camera.

Wonder why he wants the waiter to take pictures . . .

Who thinks clearly when they've been drinking?

Then he presented me with a nicely wrapped gift box.

"Happy Valentine's Day," Stelios said.

It was an average-sized box.

Hmmmm, what this could be?

Amused, I opened the box, and there was another, slightly smaller box inside, nicely wrapped as well. Curious and confused, I looked at him and then back at the box, smiling.

Okay, I'll play along with his little game.

Opening this box, inside was yet another even smaller wrapped box. I continued opening boxes until I got to a very small box.

Now, don't get excited, Ariel, it could be earrings.

Inside the last wrapped box, there was a small, dark blue, velvet box, the size of box all girls immediately recognize: the kind rings come in. Holding my breath, I opened it, and to my delight, there was a diamond, solitaire, engagement ring shining back at me.

The question every girl dreams of hearing came out of Stelios's mouth, as he leaned close and whispered, "Will you marry me?"

"Yes," I cried as I threw my arms around his neck. Meanwhile, the waiter was busy, snapping pictures of the happy occasion.

The Wedding Plans

It was exciting making all the arrangements for the wedding. I was in college at the time, majoring in foreign languages and preparing to leave soon for Paris, France, to study abroad for six months. So, most of the wedding plans had to be made a year ahead of time. It was a busy but happy season. We were to be married the following summer in the Greek church.

Stelios called and wrote often while I was away.

"I miss you terribly," he'd say. "Can I fly you home for the holidays?"

He would send flowers across the ocean, and it was all very romantic. My roommates were all envious. Oddly, I remember dreaming about all my ex-boyfriends but didn't understand why. Was my subconscious trying to tell me something?

Dreams can bring issues and fears to the surface of our conscious minds for us to process.

I returned to the United States in the winter of the next year.

That's when the arguing started.

It seemed like we were always arguing about something.

One thing we argued about was his parents. Stelios was always putting his mother's needs and concerns ahead of mine. I felt unloved and uncared for. He had not learned to leave and cleave, as the Bible says, which means putting your spouse above all others. We would argue in the car for hours. To this day, I still remember his hurtful words:

"I'll never love you as much as I love my parents."

Red flag.

Right there and then, I should have called off the engagement. But being young, naïve, and not in touch with my feelings, I ignored the gravity of the statement.

"Are you sure you want to go through with this?" Mom worried.

"The invitations have already been sent out, Ma," I said, avoiding her question. I was about to make a horrible mistake that would detour my life for the next twenty years.

Constant conflict is a red flag in a relationship. Red means STOP—do not proceed.

The Wedding Day

It was a beautiful summer day in July. The sun shone brightly, as we gathered on the lawn outside the apartment where Mom and I lived to take pictures. The bridesmaids were dressed in my favorite shade of rose pink and carried arm bouquets of white gladiolas. The ushers wore white tuxedos trimmed in burgundy. A black limousine drove us to the church in grand style.

As Mom walked me down the aisle of the church, she stopped suddenly.

"What's wrong?" I whispered.

Silence.

"Keep going, Mom."

Looking back, I feel certain that God was prompting her to tell me not to go through with the marriage.

But I did.

The deed was done, and I was married to Stelios.

The stage was set, and another drama was about to unfold.

Step to Faith: View mistakes as learning experiences rather than failures.

There is therefore now no condemnation for those who are in Christ Jesus (Romans 8:1)

CHAPTER 3

Experience Trials

Trials are a part of life. They can be very difficult at times. Until we learn to utilize the power of Faith, they usually result in stress and pressure, as we try to handle everything on our own. Sometimes, we have to hit rock bottom before we feel the need to seek help from other sources. The good news is that when the trials and tribulations of life begin to overwhelm us, we have reached a crossroad and are ready to be transported to the path to a better life.

First Signs

We decided to buy a home; or, should I say, Stelios decided we should buy a home. I was concerned about our ability to pay the mortgage.

"Don't worry. With both our incomes, we will be able to afford it," Stelios said.

"Are you sure?" I asked.

"Yes. We'll be fine in a few years."

"If you say so," I agreed with some reluctance.

We found a lovely townhome, centrally located in a nice community not far from where I grew up. It was a clean, conveniently located neighborhood, with good schools in case we ever had children.

Settling into a new home as newlyweds is usually an exciting time, when two people combine their lives and tastes to furnish a home together. The process of decorating symbolizes the two lives becoming one. In our case, it was more of a control issue than a blending of two lives.

"We don't need to buy any new furniture for the house. We can use all the things from my apartment," Stelios pronounced when we moved into our new home.

Well, maybe he's right. We really can't afford to spend extra money anyway.

One day, I came home from an art class, where I had made a macramé plant hanger. Beaming with pride, I couldn't wait to show it to Stelios.

"Look at the plant hanger I made out of macramé. Didn't it turn out nicely? Where do you think I should hang it?"

"There's no place to put that," Stelios said, completely insensitive to my feelings.

Hanging my head, I put my creation away, as the joy faded from my soul.

Maybe he'll change his mind.

The examples of control continued to manifest themselves.

"We will buy *this* washer and *this* dryer," Stelios announced while shopping for appliances with the gift money we received from our wedding.

Don't I get a say in this matter? Is he going to do the laundry?

Each time I kept my mouth shut and ignored my feelings, a little more of me died with the silence.

When involved with a controller, learn to speak up for yourself, or you will lose your self-respect.

Born and raised in a culture that dictated that a wife was to be subservient to her husband, Stelios believed a wife was not to have a say in any of the decision making and never allowed to question her husband's authority. Everything had to be his way. Foolishly, I thought because he was older, I needed to listen to him and be the submissive wife. I was too shy and timid to speak up for myself. So the cycle began again; the same as it had with my mother. Little did

I realize my self-esteem was slowly rotting away, and so was my respect for my husband.

Reliving My Past

"Hi, honey, glad you're home. I've been cleaning the house all day. How does it look?" I asked my new husband.

Stelios walked over to one of the windowsills, ran his finger across it, and asked, "What happened here?"

My feelings of pride and accomplishment were dashed in an instant, and unbeknownst to me at the time, I had married a man who had the same critical spirit as my father.

"I do not have a drinking problem," Stelios kept denying, until one night at a nightclub, he got into a drunken fight, and the entire family was promptly escorted out of the place. I was humiliated and disgusted. Over the course of several years, the argument patterns became obvious. They would coincide with Stelios's bouts of drinking.

Stelios finally conceded.

"Okay, I'll only drink one kind of liquor at a time."

Apparently, he thought that this would lessen the potency of the alcohol. He was wrong.

Stelios also smoked cigarettes. I hated the smell of them because it reminded me of my father's smoking. I didn't learn until many years later that drinking and smoking went hand in hand and were addictive behaviors.

The painful reality was that Stelios wasn't the only one who had addictive behaviors.

My Issues

"You could stand to lose some weight," a favorite high-school social studies teacher once commented.

How embarrassing to have my social studies teacher tell me I'm fat.

It stung to hear this but not enough to motivate me to change. It wasn't until I became engaged that I decided to do something about my weight. Perhaps it was the satisfaction from knowing that a man desired me enough to marry me that motivated me to take better care of myself. My goal was to lose fifteen pounds. I began exercising and was down to a svelte weight on my wedding day.

No longer did I have to wear long sweaters to cover up my ample derriere, and a new sense of confidence buoyed my spirits.

The battle was not yet conquered, however. My weight would go up and down like a yo-yo, and my happiness depended on the number on the scale each morning. This was no way to live.

Thirsty for knowledge, I read every book I could find on nutrition and tried every latest diet fad. All to no avail. Then, I came upon this suggestion: keep a daily record of what you eat and how you are feeling at the time.

You mean I have to write down not only what and when I eat, but how I'm feeling?

This was going to be a challenge, as I wasn't even aware of what I was feeling. That was the root of the problem. But I was determined to beat the battle of the bulge, and I soon realized that I was not eating out of real hunger at all but out of emotional stress and anxiety. I was using food to comfort and console me, instead of dealing with the root causes of my unhappiness.

Smoking, drinking, and overeating are all addictive behaviors that indicate some type of hidden emotional pain that has not been dealt with.

One Christmas, Stelios presented me with a membership to a local gym. I began working out and taking aerobics classes. I set small weight-loss goals and learned about nutrition and good eating habits. The weight started to come off, and I began to feel better about myself: stronger, more self-confident, and more attractive.

Things at home, however, were getting worse. Stelios's relatives were driving me crazy. His sisters were always on their brother's side. His parents did not speak English, and I did not speak much Greek, so it was very hard to discuss issues.

"They are jealous of you," my mother would say. She was supportive, but I felt more and more alone in the marriage.

One day, things finally came to a head. By losing the weight, I had gained some confidence in overcoming obstacles.

Taking control of one area of your life helps you to take control of other areas.

It's time to deal with these people.

One by one, I had a talk with each member of the family, with Stelios interpreting when needed. Though I did not speak much Greek at the time, I sat down with Stelios's parents and explained to them everything I had been thinking and feeling since we had married. I did the same with Stelios's two sisters. This was a major breakthrough for me. I was starting to stand up and speak up for myself for the first time in my life.

Although I had the courage to confront my in-laws and sisters-in-law, I still did not have the courage confront my husband. I put up with many years of verbal and emotional abuse and control from him. He belittled me and made me feel even more insecure. Since this was how my father had treated my mother, I tolerated this behavior, not realizing the mental and emotional damage that was being inflicted upon my soul which would take many years to heal.

Adult children of alcoholics tend to marry someone with addictive behaviors.

Things improved for a while after the talks but soon began deteriorating again. I decided to call it quits about three and a half years into the marriage and put a deposit on an apartment downtown, close to where I worked.

The Talk

It was time to have a talk with Stelios. Coincidently, he also wanted to have a talk with me. We sat on the living room sofa and looked at each other.

"You go first," I said to him.

"When are we going to start having children?" Stelios wanted to know.

I was dumbfounded.

He doesn't have a clue as to how miserable I am.

"I'm moving out," I announced. "I've been very unhappy for a long time, and I put a deposit on an apartment downtown."

Now it was Stelios's turn to be dumbfounded. He pleaded and begged.

"I promise I'll change," he swore to me.

Where have I heard this before?

The next day, he insisted we go downtown and get my deposit back. Obedient, I did as I was told. The sinking feeling in my stomach told me that my chance for freedom had been lost, and I didn't yet have the strength or faith in myself to follow through with my decision.

Like the trusting and hopeful young wife I was, I believed him, the same way my mother believed my father.

Actions speak louder than words.
Give people time to change before trusting them again.

Not long after that, I found out I was pregnant. Sadly, Stelios had returned to his old ways. His sweet talk and promises of change were now dim memories. Miserable and hopeless, I didn't want to tell anyone about the pregnancy.

What a mess you've gotten yourself into, Ariel. Now what are you going to do?

I finally mustered the courage to tell Stelios about the pregnancy.

"That's great news!" he exclaimed. "Wait till I tell my mother."

He had what he wanted. He was going to be a father, and that was all he cared about—regardless of the state of our personal relationship. It was up to me to try to make things work, and I was determined to do so. Little did I realize it takes two.

A Blessing Is Born

Alexi was due on the Fourth of July but decided to take his good old time and not arrive until my third day in the hospital.

Exhausted but happy to have a healthy child, I held my new baby in my arms.

What a precious miracle this child is.

Despite what everyone else said, Alexi looked like me. He had lots of dark brown hair and big brown eyes, like Mommy. He had a sweet way of holding his little clenched fist alongside his head that was so endearing.

Although unhappy in marriage, I was in love at last—with my new baby. What a blessing he was. Taking care of him was a joy, and my heart overflowed with love for him. The birth of a son brought so much happiness. Now, there was something to focus on besides the problems in our marriage.

Marriage is an institution where two people come together to joint solve the problems they never had before they got married.

Life was busy with working and the new baby, and it was about to get even busier.

> **Step to Faith:** View trials as opportunities to exercise Faith.
>
> *Consider it pure joy, my brothers and sisters, whenever you face trials of many kinds, because you know that the testing of your faith produces perseverance.* (James 1:2-3)

CHAPTER 4

Choose to Surrender

Ever feel like the pressures of life are too much to handle? Daily existence becomes a struggle, and you don't know where to turn or what to do next. You feel overwhelmed. That is when it is time to surrender.

Round Two

"I want to have another child," Stelios told me.

How will I ever be able to love another child when I love Alexi so much? And how will I be able to take care of two children, when I'm struggling enough as it is taking care of one?

My second pregnancy ended in a miscarriage while Stelios was out of town on business. Within a few months, I conceived again.

The baby was five days late, and it was the Friday before Memorial Day: another holiday weekend. I was in my doctor's office for a routine visit when the big event started.

"What's that water on the floor?" the nurse asked.

"I think my water broke," I replied in a matter-of-fact tone. The nurse ran out of the room to call the doctor, leaving me heaving and doubled over in pain.

Stelios rushed me to the hospital, as I was having what they call "precipitous labor," when the contractions start off at the peak right from the get-go.

"Get me some painkiller," I said firmly, gripping my doctor's arm.

"Not sure if we have time for that. You're already dilated."

That is not what I wanted to hear.

This time, the delivery only took forty-five minutes, barely enough time to get some anesthesia.

"He looks like Stelios," everyone said when Niko was born.

Now how can you tell that? The child just came out of the womb.

Somehow, my heart overflowed with love for this new child. He truly was a gift from God. Life with two children was busier than ever.

The Big Purchase

While I juggled my job, two kids, the cooking, the cleaning, and the other household duties, Stelios occupied himself with various and sundry hobbies.

First, he took a typing class; for what reason, I don't know. Then, he decided to teach Greek dancing to the kids at the Greek church we attended, and the latest was watching television shows about how to use other people's money to make money.

"I want to start a winery," Stelios announced one day.

"A winery?" I queried. This was something new.

"I've found a property about twenty minutes from here. From the research I've done, the soil is perfect for growing grapes," Stelios exclaimed. "The lot is fifty-two acres and is owned by a church."

"How much is it?"

He replied, "$316,000."

"Wow, that's quite a lot of money. How are we going to be able to afford to pay for it?"

"Don't worry. We can sell the property at any time and get our money back," Stelios reassured me. Trusting and believing him, we went to settlement.

Unfortunately, Stelios was wrong, and it would be years before we would be able to sell the land.

When contemplating a major purchase, be sure to do your homework.

Little did I know this was another episode of his yet undiscovered illness.

The Breaking Point

We had two houses, two cars, two children, and now two mortgages. Both of us worked full time at demanding and stressful jobs at the same company and the same department. The pressures were building.

Every night for months, Stelios would come home and complain about the problems and politics at the office. The stories he told were hard to believe, and it sounded like his boss was out to get him for some reason.

Then the crisis came.

My boss called me into his office. Stelios's boss was there as well. Both had solemn looks on their faces.

Oh my, I wonder what this is all about. I hope I am not losing my job.

"We regret to have to tell you this, but we have decided to let your husband go from the company."

I was shocked but thankful that I still had my job.

Don't overextend yourself financially. Anticipate the unexpected.

Time to Surrender

With Stelios unemployed and two mortgages, the financial pressures increased, and so did the tension in our relationship. The land was a heavy burden to bear, and one salary was not enough to carry the load.

Stelios suggested we borrow more money to continue to make the mortgage payments on the property. He spent all his time figuring out how to balance numerous credit lines while trying to find a job.

Both of us were at the breaking point.

"Can you watch the boys, so I can go to the gym?" I asked one night. Exercising was a healthy way to relieve my stress and keep my weight down.

"Can't you see I'm busy trying to juggle all these bills and creditors?" he grouched at me.

The communication between us was terse and fraught with tension. The pressures of not having a job and trying to pay all the bills and the two mortgages consumed all of Stelios's time and attention. He had little interest or patience with the kids—or me, for that matter. The stress was taking a heavy toll on both of us.

Frustrated and angry about our financial situation and deteriorating marital relationship, I searched for answers. I tried counseling, reading books from the library, and even talking to the priest from the Greek church we attended; all to no avail. I was at the breaking point, with nowhere else to turn.

Breaking points can bring us to a crisis of Faith.

One Sunday night after I put the kids to bed, I turned on the television. Alone in the basement of our townhome, I listened, as a television preacher spoke about the trials and tribulations in life. It was as if he were talking directly to me. Warm tears trickled slowly down my face, as my heart began to give up its sadness.

God understands what I'm going through. I am not alone.

I realized there was someone who cared.

And His name was Jesus.

It was time to surrender. I cried out to God and gave my life to His care and control.

"Lord Jesus, if you are really there, I give my life to you. I need you. Please help me. I don't have anyone else to turn to." A wave of peace fell over me, and I went to bed that night with a calm mind, trusting that God was with me and would take care of me from now on.

Step to Faith: Surrender my life and my will to God.

Come to me all who are weary and burdened and I will give you rest.
(Matthew 11:28-29)

No Coincidence

In the months that followed, hope replaced despair, and the seeds of faith started to grow. When I received the first issue of Dr. Stanley's monthly devotional magazine *In Touch*, I was amazed that the topic on the cover was exactly what I was dealing with at the time.

What a coincidence . . .

The next month, the same thing happened. And again, the month after that.

This is no coincidence. God is speaking to me through this man and his ministry.

I was not alone. God cared.

God had shown up and was walking with me through life. He became the father I never had, and I was so thankful.

What some call coincidences are really signs from above.

Finding God's House

At Thanksgiving, Stelios and I visited my mom, who lived out of state. On Sunday, we visited a small Bible church Mom and her husband had been attending. The pastor was teaching on the story of when Jesus was asleep in the boat during the storm and how afraid all the disciples were. Jesus woke, calmed the storm, and said, "Oh ye of little faith," to the disciples.

The pastor described how God allows storms in our lives so that our faith in Him can grow, and how the Lord knows and cares about what we are going through. Unsuccessfully, I blinked to keep the tears from rolling down my face. As I reached for a tissue in my purse, I turned to look at my mom and saw she, too, was crying. We smiled at each other through our tears in understanding of each other's pain.

When Stelios and I returned home, I knew I needed to find a new church—a church like the one I had visited, where they read the Bible and apply the principles of the Bible to real life.

There has to be more to God than sitting in a pew and watching the priest go behind the closed doors of the altar to talk to God. I need to know who God really is.

Week after week, I visited new churches and places of worship, trying to find the right one—trying to find God. I always went by myself. Stelios was not interested in attending a different church. He was perfectly content attending the Greek church. After several weeks of searching, a friend at work had a suggestion.

"Why don't you visit Trinity? It's on your side of town, and they have a lot of ministries," he explained.

Lord, help me to find you.

The following Sunday, I decided to visit the church. As I sat in the pew, listening to the choir and the congregation worship and praise God, I knew I had found a home where God dwelled.

God is here. I know God is here.

What a difference from the Greek church.

I was actually a participant and not merely a spectator, watching from the sidelines. The congregation sang, not only the choir. The people prayed, not only the pastor. The Spirit of God was there in all His glory.

For weeks and weeks, all I did was cry the entire service. It was as if the dam had burst, and all the pain and grief of my life came pouring out. The people around must have thought something was terribly wrong. But mixed with the tears of pain and grief were also tears of joy.

After all my years of hurt, suffering, and loneliness, I had finally found God.

Step to Faith: Seek and search for God.

You will seek me and find me when you seek me with all your heart.
(Jeremiah 29:13)

New Life

It was the beginning of a new life, and I was a new creation, no longer hopeless and living in despair. I knew that the Lord was with me and that He would never leave me or forsake me, as my father and my husband had.

I made a big decision. I was going to be baptized.

Now, you have to understand that in the Greek religion, you are baptized as a baby, and that is the only baptism you need. The idea behind infant baptism goes back to the Middle Ages, when babies died in infancy, and parents wanted to ensure their souls would go to heaven. In the Greek church, the event itself is a huge deal—almost like a wedding. For both our children's baptisms, we rented a hall, invited a hundred guests, and even had a band and a sit-down dinner.

In some Protestant religions, however, baptism occurs when a person is old enough to make a conscious decision to turn from their old habits and ways of thinking, and chooses to begin to live for God. It is an outward sign of an inward change, just as the marriage ceremony is an outward sign of two people becoming one. I certainly had made enough mistakes by this time to know that I needed to do things differently. Who better to turn my life over to than my omnipotent Heavenly Father?

Being baptized is a sign of obedience to God. It symbolizes the submission of my will to His which takes courage and faith. Scripture says we need to do two things: believe and take action[1] and I have learned that obedience results in great blessings.

Step to Faith: Obey God.

Blessed are those who hear the word of God and obey it.
(Luke 11:28)

It was a momentous occasion, but sadly, the only family member who came to support me was my youngest son, Niko, who was six years old at the time. The coworker who had told me about the church also attended.

"You're crazy—a holy-roller lunatic," Stelios yelled when he found out. His words cut my soul like a knife. He wasn't only rejecting my newfound faith, he was rejecting me. Another man's rejection was cutting open the old wounds my father had made many years before.

"Guess what, Yiayia? Mom was baptized today," Niko innocently shared with his grandmother.

"What? She's already been baptized as a baby! Sinful," my mother-in-law admonished. She, as well as all my Greek "friends," turned against me, but I stood my ground, continued to go to church, and took my boys to Sunday school. It had taken so many years to find God, and I wanted to give them the opportunity to know Him much earlier in life.

When you decide to seek God, prepare for opposition.

I was about to have my first lesson in faith.

Trusting God

"Enroll in the program, and we will pay for your education," the blurb in the company e-mail said. It was an opportunity of a lifetime: go to graduate school at one of the most prestigious universities in the world, all expenses paid.

Stelios is having a hard time finding a job. I should take advantage of this opportunity. Having a graduate degree might help our income in the future. I wonder what Stelios will say.

It was the last day to apply for the program. Somehow, I was able to get all the information I needed to take home and decide with Stelios that evening.

"It's only one night a week, and I can walk to the school from work. The company will pay for everything up front, including the books. It is an opportunity of a lifetime," I explained to Stelios.

"It is a good opportunity," Stelios reluctantly agreed. "Who is going to watch the kids?"

Stunned by his question, I tried to maintain my composure.

"Can't you watch them for one night?" I asked. "I'll have dinner made ahead of time, and all you have to do is feed them and help them with their homework."

"All right, go ahead and sign up." There was little enthusiasm in his response.

This decision was a big step.

Lord, if this is your will, I am stepping out in faith and trusting you to make a way for me to do this.

I was learning to look to God in the decisions in my life, and it was just in time. Everything was about to collapse.

Step to Faith: Trust I am being guided.

Trust in the Lord with all your heart, and in all your ways submit to Him, and He will make your paths straight.
(Proverbs 3:5-6)

CHAPTER 5

Focus on God's Strength

"I want to kill myself," Stelios threatened one night as he sat on the staircase inside his parents' home, a telephone cord wrapped around his neck. Forlorn and in despair, it had been days since Stelios had bothered to get dressed, and he was still in his pajamas. Seeing him sitting there on the stairs, I felt so sorry for him. I knew he was depressed, but I hadn't realized how bad the situation had become.

"We're going to the hospital to get help, and we're going now," I declared. I came home from work to find no one home, and seeing Stelios like this was quite a shock.

Seek professional help when life's pressures are overwhelming.

Stelios Collapses

We drove up the tree-lined road to the mental hospital. I'd never been to one before and was feeling a bit anxious, not knowing what to expect. The doctors evaluated Stelios and diagnosed him as being manic-depressive, or bipolar as they now call it, and admitted him into the mental hospital. They started him on several medications and kept him under strict surveillance. A person with bipolar disorder exhibits mood swings and tends to go through extremes of both positive and negative emotions, so you never know what they might do.

The diagnosis made sense of all the unexplainable behaviors I had seen over the years: the bursts of energy to start new projects, the purchase of $4,000 worth of clothing at a men's store, the purchase of the fifty-two acres of undeveloped land.

Before, I had chalked these things up to his drinking and grandiose ambitions, unaware that there was a much deeper problem lurking beneath the surface.

Watch out for unexplainable behavior: it might be sign of something more serious going on.

Here I am now—working full time, raising two small children, taking care of the house and yard, going to graduate school, and now Stelios is in the hospital, and I have to take over all the bill paying. Lord, I need your help. This is more than I can handle.

Since Stelios had lost his job, my income was not enough to pay all the bills and keep up with the payments on the property. Now, we had medical bills on top of everything else.

Stelios was in and out of the hospital, and the responsibilities for handling the bills and the creditors fell into my lap. I spent hours on the phone at work, dealing with attorneys and creditors, trying to make decisions about the finances. This was a very difficult and stressful time for me, as Stelios had always handled the finances in our marriage, and I didn't know a thing about them.

Lord, you know I need wisdom and guidance. Please help me to make the right decisions about these finances.

Step to Faith: Ask for wisdom.

If any of you lack wisdom, you should ask God who gives generously without finding fault and it will be given to you.
(James 1:5)

I clung to God tighter and tighter, reading my Bible daily and listening to Dr. Stanley on the radio every chance I got.

Stelios began to recover and was able to participate in home life again, but things were no longer the same between us. The financial pressures were too much for our unstable marriage to bear, and I had lost all respect for Stelios due to the way he treated me.

Last-Ditch Effort

"Never," I swore to myself.

"I will never be divorced. I *will* make this marriage work."

I knew that the Lord was with me, and I was hopeful that things would get better and somehow work out. What I did not realize was that human beings can only do so much through their own strength and that it takes two people committed to each other *and* to God to make a marriage work.

> *Though one may be overpowered, two can defend themselves.*
> *A cord of three strands is not easily broken.*
> (Ecclesiastes 4:12)

Already halfway through my graduate courses, there was at least one part of my life going well. The Lord took care of every issue that arose, and I was getting As in my classes.

One day, Stelios dropped a bombshell.

"I've decided to get off my medication. I don't need it." Back we went to the roller-coaster ride of depression and manic behavior. I never knew from one day to the next whether Stelios would be happy or depressed.

This reminds me of growing up with my alcoholic father.

So did the arguing. One time, things got so bad, Stelios's father had to come over to referee. I was ready to call the police. It reminded me of Mom and Dad fighting years ago.

We had been to several counselors over the years trying to work through our issues. As a last-ditch effort, we started going to a new counselor.

Lord, please show me what my part of the problems is.

The counselor interviewed each of us separately.

"I want you to be totally honest with me," I said to the counselor when he met with me.

"Tell me what you see as the major problem in our marriage."

I looked at him and waited.

"It's your husband's Greek upbringing," he said quietly.

"What?" I exclaimed. "It can't be. You mean to say the root of all these problems is that he was born in Greece?"

"Yes, I believe so."

I was at a loss as to what to do. This was something I could not change. I had learned that there is only one person I can change, and that is me. I wish the movie *My Big Fat Greek Wedding* had been out at the time. When I saw the movie on a date many years later, I noticed how the mother handled the father and said to my date, "If I had only known this technique years ago, I might have saved my marriage." He thought I was joking.

The Marriage Collapses

In October, after fourteen years of marriage, we decided to separate due to all the fighting. Everything was out of control. I was still suffering from seeing my parents fight all the time, and I didn't want my children to be scarred, as I had been.

Being a new Christian, however, the decision to separate was very difficult. Torn between wanting to separate and my Christian beliefs about holding the family together, I prayed fervently for direction. The Bible teaches that a believer should stay with the unbelieving spouse, so I decided I would continue to try to work it out with Stelios in our home.

And if a woman has a husband who is not a believer and he is willing to live with her, she must not divorce him.
(1 Cor 7:13)

However, it was not my choice to make.

"I'm moving out tonight," Stelios announced unexpectedly one night at the counselor's office.

"What are you going to tell the boys?" I asked, appalled at the lack of communication and no warning: another example of Stelios trying to control the situation.

"Shouldn't we prepare them?" I queried. Stelios agreed to stay at home a few more days before moving up to his parents and talk over how we would handle presenting it to the boys. It was a tough time for the family.

"Your dad and I aren't getting along, as you know by our fighting. So, your father is going to go up and stay with Yiayia and Papou for a while."

Stelios moved up the street to stay with his parents, and I stayed at the family home with the boys. Stelios would come over to celebrate holidays and birthdays. He and I would take long walks around the neighborhood, discussing our problems, and we continued to try the counseling routine.

Two years went by.

With no child support.

Finally, it dawned on me.

If I am going to get any child support, I am going to have to file separation papers. Lord, what should I do?

The reality of the situation was that Stelios had already divorced the boys and me physically and financially. By spending all his energy and effort on his various hobbies and moneymaking schemes, Stelios had nothing left to give to his wife and sons.

Initiating divorce proceedings was the only way to force things to a head one way or the other. I hoped that by filing for separation, the reality of the situation would somehow wake up Stelios.

Unfortunately, he had already made up his mind, and there was no turning back for him.

"I'm not the first person to be divorced, and I won't be the last," he said one evening.

It was then I knew that he had given up.

One quiet, Sunday afternoon, Stelios came by, and we sat down with the boys to have a family meeting at the dinner table.

"Boys," Stelios said, "your mother and I have decided to get a divorce."

Neither of us were prepared for the boys' reactions. Niko, who was eight years old at the time, ran screaming from the room, up the stairs to his bedroom, and slammed the door. Alexi, who was ten, seemed stunned by the reality of it all. He didn't say much, as usual, about his feelings. It was a painful day for all of us, and at that moment, I realized why the Bible says that God hates divorce. Our family was destroyed.

> *Even though I walk through the darkest valley,*
> *I will fear no evil, for you are with me.*
> (Psalms 23:4)

Mental Collapse

"So, here I am," I said to the counselor, who had been taking notes all the while.

"Sounds like you've had a rough go of things. You're going to make it through this. I recommend you start on some antidepressants to help you through this period. I agree with your boss's advice to take some time off from work. It's important to take time to grieve the loss of your marriage, and it will give the medication time to do its job."

A person can only take so much emotional stress and abuse for so long. The years of dealing with an alcoholic father, a husband who drank, working at a stressful job, taking care of two children, and financial and relationship worries had all taken their toll. It was as if my mind and body both declared a time-out. Enough was enough. The body has a way of protecting itself by shutting down when things get to be overwhelming. It is important to recognize, rather than ignore, the symptoms of depression and get help as soon as possible.

Treat depression with both medication and counseling.

Coming Out of the Dark

As the months went by, the medication and the counseling did their job. My thinking became clearer. The human mind and body are two parts of an intricately balanced system and have an amazing capacity to heal and return to homeostasis when given enough rest, time, and correct treatment.

We all need a little help to get through difficult times in our lives. Like crutches for a person with a broken leg, counseling, medication, and prayer proved to be the support I needed to work through the grief and pain of the divorce. Soon, I was able to get back to my job and my schoolwork.

The Tragedy of Divorce

Anyone who has been through divorce knows firsthand how awful it is. The consequences are long lasting, and the emotional pain it inflicts on each person involved, especially the children, is horrific. Nevertheless, the Lord is faithful to protect and defend us.

> *A father to the fatherless, a defender of widows, is God in his holy dwelling.*
> (Psalms 68:5)

It was finally time to address the divorce issues.

The divorce was nasty on every account. Stelios had moved up the street to his parents' home, since he said his health was suffering from all our conflicts. But he still felt entitled to come and go from the family home at his discretion. And for some reason, I allowed him to do this.

One day, while I was not home, he came over and cleaned out the place. He took everything he wanted. When I got home, I was shocked to find out what he had done.

I can't believe he did this. He still has to be in control.

Change the locks when you separate, and file a restraining order if necessary.

It was time to talk child support. We agreed to meet at the nearby mall, as it was a public place, so the discussion wouldn't get out of hand.

"I can pay you seventy-five dollars a month," Stelios told me with a forlorn look on his face. "I'm out of a job, and that's all I can afford."

"You must be kidding me," I said. I could not believe him. "Who can support two children on seventy-five dollars a month? Talk to my lawyer."

My husband and I divorced over religious differences.
He thought he was God, and I didn't.

Months later, the deceptions were uncovered. My attorney called me one day at the office.

"I have some news for you," she said. "I found out Stelios has been lying about being out of a job. He has been working all along, getting paid under the table."

I was disgusted yet glad I hadn't agreed to the paltry sum he had offered me months before.

In addition to lying about not working, Stelios accused me of all sorts of horrific things. Perhaps he was looking for a reason to justify the failed marriage. Whatever the reason, there are always two sides to every story. Each party has a part to play in a divorce, and each must accept their own responsibility for the failure.

I am living my worst nightmare.

Financial Collapse

But there was still more to come. It was time to address the finances. We decided to seek professional advice, since there were so many creditors.

There were two choices: try to work out a repayment plan with the various creditors or declare bankruptcy. I wanted to do the repayment plan, but the attorneys advocated declaring bankruptcy, since we owed so many people. Now that I think back on it, it was probably going to be too much work for them.

On a cold day in November, we signed the bankruptcy papers. It was my birthday.

Happy birthday, girlfriend—seven years of paying bankruptcy payments on top of everything else.

Selling the Land

Next was the issue of selling the land. The price of real estate had dropped dramatically since we had bought the property, and we could not get our money back, as Stelios had promised so many years ago. A local real estate agent told me we had overpaid for the property in the first place.

“You have no choice but to sell the property at auction,” the bankruptcy attorneys told us. I still recall the day of the auction. My divorce attorney came to oversee the proceedings.

“Sold!” declared the auctioneer. I turned to see who had bought the property and recognized a familiar face: the Realtor who had sold us the property originally. He and Stelios had become good friends, or so he had led us to believe.

Wonder what he is doing here.

To my surprise and dismay, our “good friend” was now representing one of the local neighbors, who purchased the property.

He made money on selling us the property, and now he’s making another commission on buying it.

> *"It is mine to avenge; I will repay," says the Lord.*
> (Romans 12:19)

For the next two years, it was one court case after another. Legal papers, attorney's fees, ugly meetings with lawyers, and angry letters from my estranged husband made my life miserable. The only thing that kept me going was my God and my faith.

My girlfriend at work gave me a small, framed plaque that says, "Lord, please help me through the changes in my life." It still sits on my desk today.

And He did help me.

The Divorce Is Final

In the month of August, almost four years from the day of our separation, the divorce was final.

I was free at last.

Although the court battles for child support would continue over the next several years, the letters from Stelios's attorney no longer sent chills down my spine when I saw them in the mailbox.

Lord, I know and trust that you will handle whatever is in this envelope.

Putting the divorce behind me, it was time to move on. Peace replaced turmoil at last. As I watched each obstacle in the divorce disappear, I began to see that God really was in control, and I grew in strength and in faith. I would need every ounce of both, as I embarked on my journey as a single parent.

> **Step to Faith**: Focus on God's strength instead of my problems.
>
> *The LORD is my strength and my shield;*
> *my heart trusts in him, and he helps me.*
> (Psalms 28:7)

CHAPTER 6

Learn to Be Responsible

How am I supposed to take care of everything, Lord? The house, the job, the kids, the bills, the car, the yard—all by myself? This is impossible, and I'm exhausted!

Sometimes God allows life as we know it to come to a crashing end. There is only one thing to do and that is to start over. Becoming a single parent is one of those situations. Faith in God enabled me to endure all those tough years and will help you to endure your situation as well.

> *For with God nothing is impossible.* (Luke 1:37 KJV)

The last thing I ever wanted to be was a single parent. After watching Mom struggle all those years raising Eleni and me, I vowed never to be in her shoes. Yet here I was: a single mom, raising two young boys all by myself. It was ironic and sad the way life had turned out.

Being a single parent is more than tough; it is almost unbearable at times. The burden of making all the decisions—finances, health, education, discipline—on your own with no one to bounce things off, the responsibility of raising two young children all on your shoulders, as well as always being the one to administer discipline is a load I would not wish on anyone.

Don't expect others to understand what you're going through.
It's enough that God does.

The Daily Routine

Days were long. The alarm clock would announce another busy day at 5:00 a.m. First thing in the morning was pretty much the only time I had to myself, so I would do my best to fit in a short jog to get some exercise and quiet time with the Lord.

No matter how hectic life gets, find some quiet time for yourself each day.

During those morning jogs, I talked to the Lord about whatever was on my mind. This quiet half hour gave me the strength and clarity of mind I needed to face the day ahead. I learned that God is a great listener, and I would be amazed at the answers to prayers I'd receive.

Step to Faith: Realize I am never alone.

I will never leave you nor forsake you. (Joshua 1:5)

The day-care center opened at 7:00 a.m., and we would be right there when the doors opened so I could be at work in the city by 8:00. I learned to set boundaries at work, so I could get out the door by 5:00 p.m.—just in time to battle rush hour traffic and pick up the boys by 6:00 p.m. to avoid being charged a late fee. When others in the office went out to socialize after work, I went straight home to pick up my kids.

"Why can't you boys put your things where they belong?" I would yell exasperated as I came in the front door and saw book bags, shoes, and toys strewn all over the house. A messy house was a sign of things being out of control and subconsciously reminded me of my out-of-control childhood.

From the moment I walked through the door, it would be chaos until bedtime. The kids needed attention, while I needed peace and quiet. Having a management position in a large computer software company demanded a great deal of mental concentration and focus, and I would be drained when I got home. By the end of the day, I couldn't even think straight.

The days were long for the boys as well, and by the time everyone got home, we were all tired, hungry, and cranky. There was barely enough time to make dinner, do homework, and take baths—that is, if I could get them to come in from playing outside. Among the neighborhood children, I was known as the "mom with the whistle."

Lord, if I didn't have to get up so early and drive in to work, if only I could work from home someday . . .

I prayed this prayer for years, but it seemed it would never come to pass. Telecommuting was being implemented in many companies across the country, and it would make my life so much simpler and save so much time. But my company was slow to change.

Raising Boys

When I was still married and the boys were old enough, I thought it would be a good idea to get them involved in sports. Raised in Greece, their dad had played soccer all his life, and I thought that might be a good sport to get the boys involved in and a good way for father and sons to bond.

It was a beautiful, crisp, fall morning, and the trees were ablaze with color. It was the first day of practice, and all four of us headed over to the soccer field. I was so excited, but unfortunately, Alexi was not. In fact, he was terrified. When it was time for the team to start warming up, Alexi ran. For some reason, he didn't want to play.

"He doesn't want to play. Let's go home," his dad capitulated.

"Why don't you go over and talk to him, and see what the problem is?" I asked. I wasn't ready to give up so easily. At this point, Alexi was clinging to the metal fence for dear life.

Somehow, I was able to cajole him into joining his teammates practicing soccer. I decided to sign up as a coach, hoping that would make Alexi feel more comfortable. Not that I knew anything about soccer, mind you, but they needed coaches. As it turned out, the other coach on our team was from Ireland and had played soccer many years. Luckily, he was very patient in explaining the rules of the game. Eventually, Alexi became interested in soccer, and it became a passion of his to this day.

Niko enjoyed soccer and baseball and was a good side-arm pitcher. He was on two soccer teams at once: the local recreation council and a travel team. He played defense and was the best left-footed kicker on the team. I was amazed at how he could kick that ball when it was so high in the air; perhaps he learned that kicking ability from watching his dad Greek dancing.

Playing sports required attending practice sessions, which often meant driving all over town, getting lost, and arriving home even later to make dinner. Those were long days, but everyone seemed to enjoy the activity.

I wish their father would come to some of their games.

Although it was fun watching the boys play sports, it was often lonely. All the other parents were coupled up, and there I sat on the bleachers, all by myself. I tried not to focus on the fact that I was a divorced single parent and put up a brave front and a smiling face.

It wasn't easy getting off work sometimes to catch a soccer game, but I felt it was important for at least one of the boys' parents to be present. Although I couldn't make every game, I did the best I could and hoped it was enough.

"To be in your children's memories tomorrow, you have to be in their lives today."

—Barbara Johnson

Taking Care of the Home

Weekdays were busy with sports and homework, and weekends were spent keeping up the house and the yard. I wanted my sons to have their own rooms and a yard to play in, so my spare time in the evenings and weekends was devoted to cleaning house, trimming bushes, mowing the lawn, and working on home repairs. Our small townhouse was over fifty years old, and there was always something breaking or needing attention. Although the boys helped some, the majority of the work was on my shoulders.

Turning to the church for assistance proved fruitless. The churchwomen frowned on me, because I was divorced. Shame, guilt, and condemnation were all I got from them.

"Why don't you come to Bible study?" they asked, their hair perfectly coiffed and dressed to the nines.

Because I barely have time to brush my teeth, I thought, biting my tongue.

At that time, there were no programs in place to assist single moms. I am thankful that today, perhaps through my petitions, the church has realized there is a huge need, and it has a responsibility to assist single moms. The Bible says that true religion is helping widows and orphans. A single mother is in the same situation: no husband to help provide or support her. My church now helps with home repairs and makeovers and provides used cars and food for single moms.

After the boys went to bed, it was time to sit down and do my graduate school homework. After a long day, it was tough to keep my eyes open and my mind focused on schoolwork. Sometimes the sheer pace of daily life would get to me. Disgusted and exhausted, I'd sit in the kitchen, my face in my hands, and wonder why I was so tired all the time.

Lord, I'm so tired. This is all too much for me to handle. It's like I have two full-time jobs!

My child, you do have two full-time jobs. In fact, you almost have three, because you are going to school at night. I never meant for it to be this way. You have got to save some energy for when you get home. You can't give all you have at the office. The boys need you to be calm when you get home.

It was a revelation. I was expending all my energy at the office and had nothing left for my children at the end of the day. They were the most important people in my life. It was time for a new approach.

A New Approach

The definition of insanity is doing the same thing over and over again and expecting different results. Many times, the realization that I am repeating the same behaviors has motivated me to take a new approach to situations.

With God's help, I made a conscious effort not to put all my energy into my job so that I would be calmer and less reactive when I got home. Losing my cool because the boys didn't put their book bags where they belonged or left their dishes in the sink didn't help anyone and only made matters worse.

If I want a calm home, then I have to be calm. Lord, please give me self-control, and help me to stay calm.

> *Everyone should be quick to listen, slow to speak,*
> *and slow to get angry.*
> (James 1:19)

"The mother sets the tone for the home," all the child-rearing books said.

I decided to start having weekly Bible studies at home on Wednesday nights. It was a battle most of the time to get the boys to be quiet, sit still, and pay attention, but I was determined to teach them the Bible's stories and messages and help us all memorize scripture.

"Read us another story about David and Goliath," Niko would request. David was his favorite Bible character. We all can relate to facing giants in our lives, and the life of David is a great example of how one person's faith helped him to overcome many obstacles and become king of a great nation.

Step to Faith: Read the Word of God.

So faith comes from hearing, and hearing through the word of Christ.
(Romans 10:17 CEV)

When we finished reading the book of Proverbs, I summarized the main themes, typed up all the lessons learned, and posted a copy on the wall in the kitchen, where the kids ate breakfast, so they would see it every morning. My sister gave me the idea of taping scripture verses to my kitchen cabinets. Each week, as a family, we would memorize a new scripture verse. It was fun and helped our family to keep focused. Alexi, with his brilliant mind and photographic memory, would always be the first to memorize the passage.

Slowly but surely, things started to improve around the home. There was a lot less tension in the home. I was calmer, and things ran more smoothly.

I also started going to counseling again, to talk about the issues that were on my mind: the divorce, the kids, the house, the bills, the child support, the job pressures. Venting to the counselor was like letting the steam out of a pressure cooker.

On a beautiful, spring day in May, I proudly graduated with a Master of Science degree. This was quite an accomplishment, considering everything that had been going on for the past two and a half years. With all the negative things that were going on in my personal life, once again the Lord provided something positive on which to focus. It was a bright spot against the dark clouds of divorce and financial disaster. A renewed sense of hope filled my being, and God gave me the strength to carry on.

Keep your thoughts positive because your thoughts become your words. Keep your words positive because your words become your behavior. Keep your behavior positive because your behavior becomes your habits. Keep your habits positive because your habits become your values. Keep your values positive because your values become your destiny."

—Mahatma Gandhi

Starting a Social Life

It was time to get a social life and get back to my passion for dancing.

It was in my blood, as they say. Aunt Rose, my mom's oldest sister, had been an instructor for the Arthur Murray Dance Studio for more than twenty years, and the rest of my mom's side of the family had all been good dancers as well.

Although it was an extra expense to pay a babysitter, I knew it was important to give myself a break from the job and the kids. I didn't need a partner to go swing dancing, as there were usually plenty of single men with whom to dance. One day, my friend Margie and I talked about going dancing.

"There's a swing dance on Friday nights at the Johns Hopkins campus," I shared. "No alcohol, and no smoking, either."

"I like to dance," Margie said. "It'll be fun. Let's go."

Margie was a fun gal who worked in my office. Blond hair, blue eyes, and buxom, she was the life of the party and had a knack for making people laugh. She was divorced as well and happy on her own.

"Get married again? Heck no. What do I need that for?" she quipped.

Friday night came, and off we went to the swing dance. The place was full of people, and the band was playing swing tunes. We stood, tapping our toes, and watched as the couples bounced around the floor, smiling and having fun. A few songs went by, and we were still standing there, like uninvited wallflowers. I felt like I was back in high school, waiting for someone to ask me to dance.

"You see those two guys right over there?" Margie asked.

"Yup. Are you thinking what I'm thinking?" I asked, smiling. They looked harmless enough.

"You take the one on the left, and I'll take the one on the right."

There is strength in numbers, as they say. Margie and I approached the two men, asked them to dance, and off we went. Margie was a good dancer, so was I, and that was all it took for other guys to start asking us to dance. We had a marvelous time, twirling and swirling to the sounds of '50s music. Exhausted but happy, Margie and I gathered our coats as the evening ended.

"Let's do this again next week," Margie suggested as we walked each other to our cars.

"You got it. Thanks for coming with me tonight."

It didn't take long to lose another fifteen pounds, and I began to feel like a new person: more confident, more attractive, and certainly much happier.

Make time to enjoy yourself. You'll be much happier and a better parent.

Loneliness

I climbed in my car and began the drive home.

Thank you, Lord, for a fun evening.

Then, the feeling hit. An all-too-familiar enemy would try to dampen my spirits after having a good time.

Wouldn't it be nice to have a regular dance partner? Maybe I'll meet someone nice at one of these dances . . . someday.

I could feel the smile slowly turn into a frown.

Until then, I am going to be happy right where I am.

I decided I was not going to let negative thoughts steal my joy. It was a lesson I would have to remind myself of many times before I learned it.

> *For your Maker is your husband—the LORD Almighty is his name—the Holy One of Israel is your Redeemer; He is called the God of all the earth.* (Isaiah 54:5)

Sick Kids

"Mommy, I don't feel good."

Those are words a single parent dreads hearing. Day care won't take them. It was either stay home from work or find someone else to watch them and then worry the whole day if they were all right.

A curious thing, though, is that many times, even if they wake up feeling badly, an hour or two later they are back in action, jumping all around. It's a tough call to decide whether your child is sick enough to stay home. Sometimes, the child merely wants your attention and feigns being sick. If you haven't been a single parent, you probably can't relate to this dilemma. But believe me, a sick child makes a busy morning even more challenging. I finally decided that the best approach was just to stay home from work and take care of my child. Work would have to wait, and my child needed me.

Taking Care of Myself

"After everything I do for you two!" The words were out of my mouth before I barely realized what I was saying.

Ariel, how do you think that makes these kids feel? It's not their fault that you are a single parent. Get a grip.

Whenever I heard myself say those words, or I felt like saying those words, I learned it was a sign that I was doing too much. I was caught between feeling overwhelmed and guilt.

Time to slow down and do something nice for yourself, Ariel.

These outbursts were a sign of impending burnout, and I learned to pay attention.

Taking care of yourself doesn't have to be expensive or take a lot of time. One of the best treats I gave myself was going for a run in the mornings. Before the sun was even up, I'd don my running shoes and jog over to the local college, about a half a mile from the house. It was a beautiful, quiet, tree-lined course, and I could fit in a three-mile jog in about a half an hour.

On some mornings, I would catch a glimpse of a deer or two in the woods. "As the deer pants for the water, so my soul longs after thee. You alone are my heart's desire, and I long to worship thee." The words of a favorite church song would come to mind. It felt like God was sending me a personal reminder that He was always close by. These morning jogs would refresh and energize me, and I was ready to face the challenges of the day.

Other simple things I would do for myself were to close the bathroom door and take a nice, hot, bubble bath or make myself a quiet, candle-lit dinner when the kids were at their dad's for the weekend.

A bouquet of fresh-cut flowers on the table was another inexpensive pick-me-up. I loved the scent of fresh flowers, and the colorful bouquets brightened up the room and my spirit. I didn't need to have a man in my life to enjoy flowers or have a candle-lit dinner.

Managing Money

Now that I was on my own, it was up to me to learn how to manage my money. When I was married, Stelios took care of the finances. I trusted him, and look where that got me.

"We can't afford to save anything. We have too many bills," he'd say.

"We can't afford not to save," I'd counter. "We have two kids we have to put through college. Just where do you think that money is going to come from?"

We couldn't even agree on how to handle our finances, and this caused many arguments over the years. Experts say money is one of the main issues couples fight over, and it certainly was in our case.

Growing up, I was goal oriented and developed good savings habits. I had saved money for my first car and my trip to France to study abroad in college. I decided to read some Christian books on the subject, to see what they had to say. They all said to have at least six months of expenses in a savings account, so that became my first goal. I also learned how to balance my checkbook and create a budget. Even though money was tight, it was comforting to know where I stood financially. And having money in the bank gave me a sense of security knowing that I had something to fall back on in case of an emergency or unexpected need.

Tithing

Now that I was on my own, it was imperative that I budgeted my money well. I got paid once a month, and I wanted to start tithing, something we had never done while I was married.

Lord, you know I can't afford to give 10 percent. How much shall I give?

The Lord gave me a number, and that's what I would give, faithfully and cheerfully.

> *God loves a cheerful giver.* (2 Cor 9:7)

Every January, the pastor would give a sermon on tithing.

How much should I give this year, Lord?

Each time I asked, a figure would come into my mind. It was always more than I thought I could afford, but somehow God made a way until, before I knew it, I was tithing the entire 10 percent. Now I know what you're thinking—10 percent is a lot of money. But it is really not about the money. It is about faith and trust. God will more than make up for the 10 percent we tithe. Tithing makes me realize that my earnings are a blessing and a gift from God and I am only a steward of His resources.

It was a good feeling to know I was being obedient to the Lord, and God blessed me in many ways because of my faithfulness and trust in Him.

Saving

It was also important to have something in the bank "for a rainy day." Every month, I would put fifty dollars away in a savings account at my credit union, which gave the best interest. I also put part of the child support money in a savings account for my sons for their college education. Slowly, month by month, year by year, the accounts grew. This meant having to do without some things—not buying brand names and not going out to eat as often—but we had a comfortable life, and the children learned to appreciate what they had. Christmas was not a department store extravaganza, as it is in some families, but Alexi and Niko realized the value of a dollar.

A well-known motivational speaker, Jim Rohn, talks about a kid and a dollar. He advises to teach children not to spend the whole dollar. In one of his CDs on leadership, he quips:

Take your children on a trip to the poor side of town. Tell them that's where people live that spend the whole dollar. In case you already live there, just show them around.[1]

It is so important for children to learn the value of money at an early age and not to take things for granted. We all work very hard, and God calls us to be good stewards of what He has entrusted to us.

Now that our home life was under control, it was time to get the house in order.

Step to Faith: Take responsibility for my actions, thoughts, and feelings.

But let each one examine his own work, and then he will have rejoicing in himself alone, and not in another. For each one shall bear his own load.
(Gal 6:4-5 NKJV)

CHAPTER 7

Let Your Life Be Transformed

This place is in a total shambles.

After years of neglect, our nice, little townhome was a complete mess. As I regarded the jungle that was our backyard, a bittersweet smile crept across my face. The neglected state of the house was a sad reminder of the neglected state of my life. Although my marriage was over, life was not.

It was time to rebuild and start again.

Time to Rebuild

Ariel, you have to get this place in order.

The house repairs and maintenance had always been Stelios's domain, but he had not done much around the house for the past several years. Our small townhome was over fifty years old, and things were breaking all the time. Since we separated, he never once offered to fix anything, despite the fact that this was the home of his two children. So here I was, a single mom, not knowing a thing about home maintenance.

Yet, I was determined to learn.

It was time for a plan. After making a list of all the things that needed to be repaired, replaced, painted, or fixed, I made a plan to tackle each one, saving as much as I could each month to pay for them.

Recognize that overwhelm is not real. It is a feeling based on fear that there's too much to do and not enough time to do it. Prioritize and focus on one thing at a time.

First Things First

The windows were the first things that needed replacing. The gaps between the windows were so wide that I could see outside. To keep the cold air from coming in, I had to put plastic sheets over the windows in the winter. The windows reminded me of the boundaries in my life.

A boundary is a dividing line, or border, identifying where one property ends and another begins. Within the human context, boundaries define where one person ends and another begins. We all need boundaries in our lives. Boundaries help us identify what we will allow into our lives and what we will not. They also help us to realize what is our responsibility to protect and what is another person's responsibility.

Our time, money, energy, and physical selves all need protection, just as the walls of a castle protect the inhabitants and windows keep the cold air out and the warm air in. It was time to repair and strengthen my boundaries to keep harmful things and unhealthy relationships out of my life and let good things and safe relationships in.

The windows downstairs were in the worst shape. Replacement windows are not cheap, so I saved enough money to replace the downstairs windows first. The next year, I replaced the windows upstairs. At last, there was quiet in the home, both literally and figuratively, and my boundaries, like the windows, were slowly being replaced with newer, better, and stronger ones.

Tearing Down

The previous owners liked the colonial, early American-style decor. Busy wallpaper was everywhere. Ugly, dark, wooden beams hung obtrusively from the ceilings, and a horrid, wagon-wheel light fixture adorned the dining room.

When Stelios first showed me the house, I told him I would only move in if we got rid of the wood beams, and he promised we would. Twenty years later, they were still there. The dark, wooden beams were a reminder of Stelios's broken promises to me, and I couldn't wait to get rid of them.

One day, a contractor came over to the house to give me an estimate for taking down the beam. "You really want to get rid of these, don't you?" he asked.

"Yes, I certainly do," I replied emphatically.

Right then, he reached up, grabbed one of the beams, and yanked it down. I was elated and amazed. "All these years, I thought they were real wood."

"Nope, Styrofoam," he replied.

It took him only a few minutes to tear down all the beams and pitch them out to the trash. Something deep within was set free.

The Colors of Bright

The walls of the house were painted a drab shade of beige.

It's time to spruce up these walls and get some color in here.

I chose a light, peachy-pink shade to brighten up the place, but first I had the daunting task of taking down all the old wallpaper. This proved to be no easy process. Every evening after dinner, I soaked and scraped the wallpaper to get it down. It was supposed to be an easy job if it came off in sheets. But it didn't, and the job was painstakingly long and tedious.

Finally, the hard part was finished. Now it was time for the fun.

A friend from work and her husband came over to help paint the dining room. I couldn't wait to take down the old wagon-wheel light fixture that had been hanging over the dining room table for years. The ceiling had glue circles about three to four inches in diameter all over from where the ceiling tiles had been.

It was quite an ordeal for my friend's husband. He spent days sanding down the circles, trying to get them to disappear. I could see he was getting frustrated.

One day, I went to Montgomery Ward, where I spotted a beautiful, glass chandelier that was on sale.

This would be perfect in the dining room.

When I got home, I showed off the new chandelier. The reflections from the light would hide any imperfections in the ceiling. We were both relieved.

My girlfriend came over, and together, she and her husband put up the border for me. He even covered the outlet covers with the new border to match. It was so nice to see them working together as a couple, side by side.

Out with the Old

Next, it was time to redo the living room. The furniture was old, and everything was either from Stelios's old apartment or from deceased relatives. Most of it was not my taste at all. For months, I shopped and saved for the leather sectional sofa I had always wanted. The purchase was a big step for me. All the years I was married, the only new furniture Stelios ever allowed me to buy was a set of bedroom furniture.

It was the perfect sofa, made from soft, Italian leather. It had to be special-ordered, and I decided on pearlized oyster, a glimmering shade of beige. The saleswoman showed me some beautiful, multicolored pillows that would accent the sofa.

They're expensive, but oh, what the heck. You only buy a sofa once.

I went ahead and ordered the pillows to match. It was too exciting.

Next, it was time to tackle the carpet. It was over twenty years old and spotted and stained from the previous owners' dog. Every night after dinner, I would get down on my hands and knees and work on pulling up the carpet. Pulling it up was the easy part. Then came the hard part: taking out the nails and pulling up the tack strips.

What a thrill it was when the boys and I finally rolled up the heavy carpet and heaved it into the trash. "Another job over and done with, boys," I said as I sighed with relief and shook the dust off my hands.

Now, I'm free of that, too!

The next step was to refinish the wood floors. When the workers finally left days later, the floors gleamed. The new sofa was in place, and the walls were painted. I stood and gazed at my beautiful, new living room. Slowly but surely my house was being transformed.

Ms. Fix-It

One room at a time, I completed the house repairs and turned into Ms. Fix-It. I learned how to replace the gadget in the toilet, fix the toilet handle that had been loose for years, and get hairs out of the drains using a snake. Overcoming my fear of heights, I learned to climb a ladder to clean out the gutters and downspouts and paint the shutters.

Niko showed me how to start the lawn mower and to use a hedge trimmer. An old boyfriend taught me to check the oil in my car and the air in my tires. I learned about the fan and the bees in the attic the hard way.

The bedrooms were painted and the bathroom remodeled. Now, it was time to tackle the kitchen.

In with the New

The kitchen had been remodeled when we first moved in, but that was twenty years ago. It was old, outdated, and dark. There wasn't enough counter space, and I hated the colonial wallpaper.

It took over two years to decide how to remodel the kitchen, yet it was well worth the time and energy I put into it.

"This is so exciting," I said as the installer hung the new cabinets. "Let me take a picture of you." He must have thought I was nuts, but it was a momentous occasion. Glossy, white cabinetry replaced the old, dark, wooden cabinets. A fresh coat of paint brightened up the walls where the colonial wallpaper had hung. Since I love to cook, I increased the counter space as well as the size of the breakfast nook. The best part was that I had saved up enough money to pay for it all in cash—no debt or loans to hang over me for years to come. My savings habits were paying off well for me after all.

Lord, thank you for this kitchen. You know how much I love to cook. Thank you for allowing me to be able to save and design this kitchen the way I've always dreamed.

The last room in the house to be redone was the basement. By this time, the boys were old enough to help paint, but they got bored after one day of painting. So, there I was again, every night painting the wood paneling. A colorful, new carpet replaced the old, green carpet, and a navy, leather sofa and chair made the basement a perfect space for the boys to watch television, relax, and hang out with their friends. That Christmas, I bought a foosball table that gave us many hours of family fun. It was the perfect gift to begin our new life.

A House and a Life Transformed

At last, the house was in order.

This house is taking on a new life. Peaceful, beautiful, and full of light; and so is my life.

The slow but steady transformation of our home was symbolic of the transformation in our lives: from chaos, turmoil, and darkness to peace, ease, beauty, and light. God is faithful to transform us, if we let him.

He begins by transforming our minds and our thoughts. As I got rid of old furniture and old items that I no longer needed, I also got rid of old patterns of thinking that no longer served me. As I purchased new furniture and items, I also acquired new ways of thinking.

It takes time, but God is patient with us, and so we must be with ourselves. As I was slowly transforming the rooms of our home, God was at work on the inhabitants as well.

There was one thing, though, that I had been waiting on for years and needed desperately.

Step to Faith: Allow God to change me.

Therefore, if anyone is in Christ, he is a new creation.
(2 Cor 5:17 ESV)

CHAPTER 8

Learn to Wait

Waiting can be difficult, especially when you're waiting for something you really need. Believe me, waiting on God is the best thing you can possibly do, because He rewards faith and trust with great blessings.

Praying for Years

For years, I had been praying for a new car, but being a divorced, single mother of two small boys, I could hardly afford a new car. Many times, I had said to the boys in faith, "When God is ready for us to have a new car, He will provide one."

The little, white Ford Mustang had served me well, since Stelios and I purchased it off the lot more than fifteen years before. I liked it, because it was white and resembled a sports car.

It was paid off, which was good, but in the last few years, there was always something going wrong with it that cost me money—money I could not afford to spend.

Transmission, Oil Leaks, and Breakdown

First, it was the transmission; that was a big expense. Then there was the oil leak. Next, it needed new tires. Now, the carburetor was blowing up under the hood, literally, catching on fire.

Trying to find a reputable mechanic who didn't see dollar signs when I walked in was no easy task. As soon as I started asking questions, I could tell what they were thinking by the looks on their faces.

Single female, knows nothin' 'bout cars.

I was at their mercy, and they knew it.

When the car needed to go to the shop, it was such a hassle. I had to get the kids to day care by 7:00 a.m., rush to be downtown at work by 8:00 a.m., and dash home to get to the daycare center to pick up the boys before 6:00 p.m.—all with no car.

The last straw came when I took the car in for the carburetor problem. When the shop called to tell me my car was ready, a wave of relief washed over me.

I hope this will be the last of these car repairs.

Sadly, as I was driving to work the next day in expressway traffic, my little Mustang began to slow down.

Something must be wrong. Now what?

As the little mustang slowed even more, I navigated to the right lane and decided to pull onto the shoulder. The car came to a dead stop.

Just great. They must have messed up something at the shop.

Thankfully, I had recently purchased a cell phone (which had just come out in the market), "in case of an emergency." I had debated long and hard about whether I could afford one, but now I was glad I had decided to get one.

Well, this certainly constitutes an emergency.

After calling for a tow truck, I waited on the expressway, as the morning rush hour traffic zoomed by. I felt alone and helpless. "I am so glad to see you," I exclaimed as the tow truck driver pulled up behind me not too long after.

"Yes, ma'am. I can see you need help. Can I give you a ride to your office?"

Several hours late, I arrived at my office.

"Where have you been? We've been worried about you," my coworkers asked. It was not like me to be late to work.

"My car broke down on the highway, but I'm okay."

Thank goodness, the kids weren't in the car this time.

An Answer to Prayer

One night soon after the breakdown, my aunt Rose and I were sitting in church for a special evening service. I related to her the harrowing episode on the Beltway.

"That car you're driving is too dangerous for you and the boys to be riding around in," she admonished. "Go out and look for something you like, and I'll buy it for you."

I could hardly believe my ears.

"Thank you, Aunt Rose!" I said as I threw my arms around her and gave her a big hug.

She was an answer to prayer.

Answers to prayer may come from an unexpected source.

Car Shopping

After checking *Consumer Reports* and doing my research, I decided on a Subaru wagon. It had plenty of space for groceries, kids, and luggage. It was reliable and had all-wheel drive, which was good, since we lived in Baltimore and got a lot of snow some years. And it got good gas mileage.

Not particularly sporty, but hey, I'm a mom. A sports car will have to wait.

One Saturday morning, Aunt Rose and I visited the Subaru dealership.

I had two wishes. I really wanted a CD player and a sunroof. We looked over the lot and finally decided on a Subaru wagon. I loved the spruce green color. The car had a CD player, but no sunroof.

"How much to add a sunroof?" I asked the salesman.

"A thousand dollars," he replied. I wondered if I could save up the extra thousand dollars to get one added.

"We'll have to think about it," Aunt Rose said to the salesman as we walked off the lot. I had a sinking feeling she was not particularly happy about the price of the car, but I didn't say anything. I couldn't help but be disappointed after all the excitement of getting a new car.

"Well, I guess it just wasn't meant to be. It must not be God's timing." I tried to console myself. It had been so long already.

"I'll call you in a few days," Aunt Rose said as we parted.

A few days later, I received a call at work. It was Aunt Rose, telling me that the price of a new car was more than she wanted to spend. "Would you be interested in looking for a used car?" she asked.

"Sure," I said. "Anything would be better than what I have now."

Used Cars Are Good

Right away, I got out the Yellow Pages and started calling the used car dealerships in town. Apparently, Subarus are good cars, and there weren't many used ones available at that time. Finally, I found a dealership that had one on the lot.

"Tell me about the car," I said to the man on the phone.

"Well," he said, "it's a 1995 wagon. It has seven thousand miles on it. It has a three-year warranty, and it's the only one I have."

"Can you tell me what color it is?" I asked expectantly.

"Spruce green," replied the salesman. "And, oh, by the way, it has a CD player." He paused for a moment and then added, "And a sunroof."

I was stunned. It had everything I wanted. After saying a short prayer of thanks, I told the man to hold it for me and that I would come by to look at it that evening. I could barely contain my excitement. I knew right then that this was the car the Lord wanted me to have.

Aunt Rose and I went out that very evening to look at the car. The test drive was particularly fun because of the pickup the car had, unlike my little Mustang, which could barely pick up enough speed to get on the highway.

"What do you think?" Aunt Rose asked.

"I love it. What do you think?"

"We'll take it," she said to the salesman.

"What a blessing you are, Aunt Rose," I exclaimed, hugging her tightly. I couldn't believe I was actually getting the car of my dreams after all these years of patiently waiting.

It was time for more faith lessons in another area of my life, which would prove to be even more difficult and much more painful.

Step to Faith: Learn to wait on God if I want his best.

For since the world began, no ear has heard, and no eye has seen a God like you, who works for those who wait for him!
(Isaiah 64:4 NLT)

CHAPTER 9

Learn to Be Humble

Many times we think we are so smart and that we know everything; that is, until we face situations that are beyond us. It's bound to happen sooner or later. Then we get to learn the lesson of how to be humble.

There are several facets to humility, and the term is often misunderstood. Humility does not mean being a doormat or subjugating oneself to abusive authority. It does not mean weakness, lack of courage, or allowing ourselves to be taken advantage of.

Humility is the opposite of pride, which says we think we are better than everyone else. Humility means thinking more of others and less of ourselves. A humble attitude results in not having to have the last word in every argument, letting someone else be right, and keeping our mouth shut occasionally.

Humility also means surrendering to God's will, despite sometimes painful circumstances. When we submit our lives to God, we are admitting that He knows more than we do, which is the truth. This is not always a comfortable place to be, because we like being in control, but God orchestrates our circumstances to make us more like Jesus.

> *Take my yoke upon you and learn from me, for I am gentle and humble in heart, and you will find rest for your souls.* (Matt 11:29 NLT)

The Way It Was

Remember when you were a teenager? Things have only gotten worse since then.

Much worse.

There are many reasons for this. Due to the increasing number of unwed, single, and divorced parents many children are emotionally wounded and act out in a variety of ways: using drugs and alcohol, overeating, and overachieving, to name a few.

Many fathers are physically or emotionally absent from the home and have abdicated their responsibility to teach children values such as respect for women, respect for authority, and respect for themselves and others.

Then, there's the temptation to have the latest cell phone, iPod, iPad, or video game, which creates some real challenges for family budgets these days. On top of that, many kids also have an attitude of entitlement and assume that the world owes them a living without them having to put forth any effort whatsoever.

It is especially tough when you are a single parent, with no help or support from the other parent. I learned it was important to clearly define my values, communicate them to my kids, and stick to them, because the constant pressure from the outside world leads straight down the path of materialism and instant self-gratification. Many times, I would hear:

"Well, so and so got a new . . ." or, "Mike doesn't have to be in by ten o'clock."

My answer would always be the same.

"Well, go and live with Mike then. These are the rules of this house, and as long as you live under my roof, I expect them to be obeyed."

No matter what others around you may do, stick to your values.

The struggles kids go through during the transition from childhood to adulthood are stressful for both parents and teenagers.

Hang in there. Love them where they are, and everyone will grow through it eventually. We are all in process and on our own time frame, but God is faithful to sustain us all through the journey.

The Oldest Son

My oldest son, Alexi, is brilliant. From an early age, I could tell he was a very bright child, and his teachers told me he had a photographic memory.

"Look, Mom, look at this! I got a hundred on my test," Alexi said one day after coming home from elementary school. It was a test on the continent of Africa, and he had correctly identified every country on the continent.

"That's amazing, honey. You are a very smart little boy."

Wow, this child has a great mind.

I knew then that God had great plans for him.

He had no problem not studying, or studying very little and then getting As on his exams. Year after year, I would say to him, "Honey, you need to learn how to study better. Things aren't always going to be this easy." Year after year, he ignored my warnings, because he could always handle the work.

Alexi made friends easily, and I noticed that his best friends were often of another ethnic background or religion, such as Chinese, Muslim, or Jewish.

Thank you, Lord, that Alexi has learned we are all equal in your eyes.

Stubbornness Is as Rebellion

"I'm not going to Sunday school," Alexi asserted.

"Yes, you are. You will do what I say," I countered.

"I don't want to go!"

"Why don't you want to go?"

Back and forth we went, Sunday after Sunday. Alexi was in third grade, and I was determined that he go to Sunday school to learn about God. Without a husband to back me up and make him go, I was powerless—or, at least, that's how I felt at the time.

It was more than a battle of the wills. It was a battle for his soul.

"All right, all right, all right. I've had enough of this battling with you. Do you want to come with me to the big church instead?"

"Okay, I will go to the big church with you," Alexi consented.

I never understood what the problem was, and he never told me. We had reached a compromise of sorts. I now knew I had a strong-willed child, and the battles between us had only begun.

Pick your battles with your child,
and let them make some of their own choices.

Many Talents

Alexi was involved in many extracurricular activities at school and loved playing soccer and the trumpet. I was very proud of him and amazed that God had given me such a talented and gifted child.

At the fifth-grade graduation awards ceremony, every time they called his name to receive an award, my eyes would fill with tears of pride. I was barely able to steady the camera to capture the moment.

If they call his name one more time, I'm going to lose it.

He received so many awards and accolades. I was overcome with pride, joy, and a certain sense of relief.

Well, I haven't done so badly at being a single mother, after all.

Then, he started middle school, and his attendance record was outstanding. He was always on the honor roll. Things were going pretty well, until Alexi began high school and hit the teenage years.

Then the rebellion began.

Raising a Teen

As Alexi approached the teen years, the battles of the will increased. Little things like taking out the trash and turning off the computer or the video game became major arguments between us. We were both stubborn in some ways, but I was the mother, and he still lived under my roof.

"What's wrong?" I would ask.

"Nothing," would be the usual reply. Yet, Alexi's downcast look and cold demeanor told me otherwise.

"It is important to express your feelings," I cajoled for years. But to no avail. He would explode over the simplest question or request, and I would have no idea what was really bothering him. Over the years, the conflicts and lack of open communication pulled us further apart and caused hurt feelings on both sides.

One day, the lack of cooperation and disrespect got to me.

"I'm sending you up to your father's for a few days, till you learn how to respect me," I announced in exasperation.

"He has to write the sentence 'I will respect my mother at all times,' one thousand times before I will take him back," I told his father.

It took a few days, and I don't know what happened at his dad's, but Alexi wrote the sentences. It was a small victory, but it was a step in the right direction.

Disciplining a teenage boy is difficult, particularly when there is a lack of a good male role model. I tried it all: counseling, reading parenting books, and seeking advice from other parents and teachers. I even went so far as to ground him from field trips with his music group at school, which made Alexi very upset. I tried my best to be both mother and father but had to resign myself that this was an impossible feat.

According to experts at the Child Development Institute, emotional maturity is a learned ability. The National Center for Children in Poverty attributes a negative disregard for authority to a lack of emotional development in a child's early years. (*Emotional Development in the Early Childhood Years,* by Linda Ray, Livestrong.com). It is important to learn respect for authority, and I did everything I knew to get him to learn this lesson.

"If you don't learn these lessons here, God is going to teach them to you out in the big, bad world, and you can believe it's going to be a lot harder lesson for sure." God never gives up on us, but He is more interested in our character than our comfort.

When your child doesn't obey you while living at home, know that God will keep teaching him when he moves out.

Sibling Rivalry

"How come you always do more for Niko?" Alexi asked annoyed.

"I love you both the same, Alexi," I told him. "What I do for one, I do for the other. There are no favorites in this house." Alexi did not seem to believe me for some reason.

Wonder why Alexi thinks I do more for Niko.

"It is true that your brother and I get along better," I explained one day, "because his personality is more like mine. But that doesn't mean I love you any less. We just have to work harder at our relationship, that's all. I love you, honey. You are my firstborn child."

It seemed that Alexi kept things bottled up for long periods of time, but when he finally opened up and got some answers, he felt better.

To me, Alexi was a lot like his dad in temperament and thinking. We just didn't seem to be able to connect. I was frustrated and at wit's end on what to do.

"You've got to remember," my counselor would point out, "Alexi is not his father, and you have had much more influence on him than his dad has." But the fact remained that Alexi had missed out on having a good father figure to help him develop emotionally, and there was nothing I could do to change that.

I made up my mind that I would learn how to deal with him. He was, after all, my son, and I desperately wanted us to get along. Eventually, I would have to give up the fight.

College Decisions

It was time to start looking for a college. I had no idea how I was going to afford to put Alexi through college and lifted the entire situation up to God and stepped out in faith again.

We visited colleges both in the area and out of state. Alexi had his heart set on Penn State. It was a beautiful school, and Alexi received early admission. He was so excited, but his joy soon turned to disappointment when he was not accepted into the honor group for which he had applied. Yet, he still wanted to go.

"How much is the tuition to go to Penn State?" I asked, certain it was going to be very expensive.

"Twenty-five thousand a year," Alexi answered.

It was time to have a heart-to-heart talk about the college expenses.

"Alexi, the reality of our situation is that we only have one salary: mine. We would have to save $2,000 a month for you to go to Penn State. Can you think of a way we can do that?"

"Not really," Alexi said.

"If you want to go to Penn State, you need to start applying for scholarships, loans, and grants. Even so, you will probably be in a lot of debt when you graduate. It's up to you. My suggestion is that you apply to three colleges, both in and out of Maryland, because you stand more of a chance at getting a scholarship to an in-state school."

Reluctantly, he agreed.

Ask and you shall receive.
Seek and you will find. Knock and the door shall be opened.
(Matthew 7:7)

A Miracle from God

One day, Alexi received a letter in the mail.

"Guess what, Ma?" he asked after reading the letter.

"What is it, honey?" I asked.

"I got a full scholarship from UMBC," he replied in a nonchalant tone of voice.

I couldn't believe my ears. This was an excellent school, and a full scholarship was truly a miracle from God.

"It includes room and board, too," Alexi explained.

"Do you realize what a miracle and blessing this is from God?" I asked Alexi.

I was ecstatic. I knew that God had heard and answered my prayers. Alexi would be able to go to college. Alexi, however, was not particularly thrilled.

"You want me to go to UMBC, don't you?" he asked me one day. His glum look showed his disappointment at realizing he probably wasn't going to be able to go to his dream college, Penn State.

"Honey," I replied in the tenderest tone I could muster, "I want you to go wherever you are going to be happy. I want you to realize if you choose to go to Penn State, you are going to have a lot of debt when you graduate. It is totally your decision, and I'll help you in any way I can."

Starting College

Alexi decided to accept the scholarship from UMBC. It was just in time for the two of us, because tensions in the home were mounting. It was time for Alexi to experience the world on his own.

"Here's my new dorm room, Mom," Alexi said excitedly as he showed me his new living quarters. "My friend from high school is my roommate. He's also the floor captain."

"You are so blessed. I never had the opportunity to live on campus when I was in college. I had to commute back and forth every day. This is so cool. It's very nice, clean, and you have a good roommate," I replied, happy that there would be a stable influence in his immediate vicinity. The two seemed to be a good match.

Once school began, I didn't hear or see much from Alexi. I chalked it up to the fact that he was busy with schoolwork and adjusting to the new lifestyle. Whenever I asked how school was going, he would give me the same answer.

"Fine, Ma. Don't worry about it."

One night toward the end of his second year, Alexi was home for a visit. I was resting in bed, getting ready to go to sleep, when Alexi decided to open up.

"I don't think I did very well on my last exam," he said in a dejected tone.

"How much did you study?" I inquired. It was a simple question but not too empathetic I admit, and it must have gone right to the heart of the problem. Minus one for Mom.

"I'm leaving," Alexi announced in a huff and bolted out of the house.

Wow, he's really upset about something. Wonder what made him react like that?

Several months later, I found out the reason Alexi was so upset that night.

A Humbling Experience

Too much partying with his fraternity brothers and not enough studying took their toll. My warnings that things were going to get harder had finally become a reality, but it was too late. The warnings had gone unheeded, and there was a price to pay. Alexi had lost his scholarship by doing poorly on that last exam.

When I heard the terrible news, I was shocked, disgusted, disappointed, and extremely sad. I was so upset that I almost canceled my plans to go out with my friends that weekend, but I decided to go to cheer myself up. My favorite band was playing at a restaurant in the city, and listening to them would help me forget my sorrows—at least for a short while. Out of the blue, a man walked up to me and said, "Everything okay with you? You look a little down this evening."

The impact of Alexi's loss was heavy on my soul, so I shared the sad tale with him.

"How many years did he make it through school?" the man asked.

"Two."

"Well, mine only made it through one year," he said quietly. "He did the same thing: lost his scholarship."

"Wow, so the same thing happened to you," I exclaimed.

This has to be God. He is trying to make me feel better by sending someone who dealt with this same situation. Perhaps He is also trying to heal this man as well.

Somehow, we were able to make a joke about the whole thing and chalk it up to growing pains. It's tough as a parent to watch your child make poor choices, but what can you do?

God loves us even when we make poor choices. Love your child the same way.

Step to Faith: Trust the Lord with my children.

And I will pour out my Spirit on your descendants, and my blessing on your children. They will thrive like watered grass, like willows on a riverbank.

(Isaiah 44:3-4 NLT)

When It Rains, It Pours

Not only had he lost his scholarship, Alexi was also deep in credit card debt. He had never been one for holding onto money. It was a family joke that "Money burns a hole in Alexi's pocket."

Alexi was also drinking heavily, and I was very concerned about his drinking and driving.

"How would you feel if you killed someone?"

"I don't care," Alexi replied.

I was mortified.

"You'll have to live with that the rest of your life," I warned him.

God Intervenes

One night, the ringing of the phone jolted me awake.

"Alexi is in jail," Niko said calmly.

Apparently, the police had pulled him over for having a broken taillight, and the officer noticed his car insurance had expired.

God is giving Alexi time in the slammer to think about things.

My own son had landed in jail. I was disgusted and certainly didn't feel like bailing him out.

He needs to sit in there until he gets his head back on straight.

God Comes Through Again

Lord, please handle this situation with Alexi. I have no idea what to do or how to handle this.

God is so merciful, and He hears our cries for help.

As it turned out, I didn't have to do anything: God took charge of the situation. The mother of Alexi's best friend had connections at the court and knew the judge. She was able to pull some strings, and in a day or two, Alexi was out of jail. Once again, I was amazed at how God takes care of things when I don't know how.

> *Do not be anxious for anything, but in all things, with prayer and supplication with thanksgiving let your requests be made known to God and the peace of God, which surpasses all understanding shall guard your hearts and minds through Christ Jesus.*
> (Phillipians 4:6-7 ESV)

"Do you realize what an act of God this is?" I asked him when he got home.

Alexi just shrugged.

The short stint in jail didn't seem to impact Alexi at all. It wasn't long after that he received a DUI.

Now, we not only had the college and financial issues to deal with, we also had to contend with court cases.

It was a difficult time for the whole family. I didn't know what to do or how to handle the situation, but I prayed to God for direction. We held regular family meetings, trying to decide on the best approach to all the problems. Alexi was in a mess in every way. He sat on my sofa, his head down and the spirit of shame upon him.

"I know I got myself into this mess, but I don't know what to do to get myself out."

"I know this is a rough time for you, honey, but you will get through this. God has a plan for your life. God will show us what to do." I tried to encourage him the best I knew how. My words were to encourage me as much as to encourage him. It was another lesson in trusting God.

Sometimes God stops our progress in life to get our attention and to teach us some things.

We decided that he needed to take time off from school to get his life in order. We made a plan for him to repay his debts. His father and I chipped in to help him pay off some of them, and he worked to pay off the rest.

I didn't want to completely bail him out, because I wanted him to learn from his mistakes.

Alexi seemed hopeful, though, and realized the error of his ways. He developed a budget, got a job, and started working full time. He began to work himself out of debt and curtail his drinking.

It was soon time for Alexi to return to college. What a great day that was.

"This is a loan, not a gift. I want you to finish your education. I'll pay half if your father pays half."

I remember going to the bank with Alexi to get a check for the tuition money.

He was thrilled, and so was I. We had come through a lot, and I think that brought us closer.

He would not be living in the dorms this time around, but he had found a place to stay with some friends. He was back at school and excited about finishing his degree. We all made it through the crisis and came out on the other side. It was truly a humbling experience for both of us. I learned that I can't solve every problem on my own and need to depend on God more than on my own abilities. When we take our cares to the Lord and admit our need for him, he is gracious to step in and help.

Step to Faith: Admit I don't have all the answers.

God opposes the proud but gives grace to the humble. (1 Peter 5:5 ESV)

Now, it was time to battle for my youngest.

CHAPTER 10

God Is on Your Side

Have you ever felt like you're in a war zone? I have. Sometimes, it seemed like every day was a battle, especially when I was raising teenagers. Rest assured, we don't have to fight the battle alone. God is on our side, and He will get us through these tough times. I know it might not seem like it today, but remember: having faith means believing in a positive outcome that we can't yet see, as well as trusting God to fight our battles along with us.

The Youngest Son

The battle for Alexi was subsiding just as another battle was brewing. Niko was having his own problems. It took quite a while to figure out what was going on, but eventually, the truth was revealed, and it was time for action.

Niko had been a happy, loving, and obedient child. We were very close, and although everyone said he looked like his dad, his personality was similar to mine. Niko was artistic and creative. He played the drums in middle school and had great rhythm. I loved watching him perform in the band probably as much as he loved playing. Growing up, I had always had an affinity for drummers, and it was interesting that God had given me a son who liked to play the drums. Niko and his brother would jam in the basement, with Alexi on his trumpet and Niko on his drums. It was great to have two musicians in the family.

Niko was also a natural athlete. He excelled at soccer and baseball. I enjoyed watching him pitch side-arm at the Little League games and kick the soccer ball with his left foot. Niko had a great future ahead of him, and I was thankful that God had given me two such wonderfully talented sons.

High School Years

"Can you have a talk with him, Coach? I don't know what's gotten into him."

When Niko was about fifteen years old, he began to lose interest in soccer. Then, his grades started dropping, and I found out he wasn't handing in his homework assignments. In the mornings, it was tough to get him up and out of bed.

His attitude changed, and Niko became a different person: very rude and disrespectful.

Who is this kid? Is this a teenage thing?

Niko was turning into someone else, like he was having an "out-of-body" experience. And to tell the truth, I did not like this new person one bit.

Pay attention to disturbing changes in your teen's attitude and behavior.

When Niko turned sixteen, things got so bad I had to resort to calling the police to get him to get up and go to school.

He needs to respect authority, and maybe the police will scare him into cooperating.

Niko, however, was indifferent and had a consistently bad attitude. He stopped playing soccer altogether, which shocked me, because it had always been his passion.

Maybe he's drinking. I'm going to wait till he gets home and smell his breath.

"Have you been drinking?" I asked one night as I got right up in his face.

"Get away from me," Niko retorted angrily, pushing by me to go upstairs.

He's hiding something. What could it be?

The Discovery

One night, the three of us were in the basement watching television. Niko had gone upstairs to go to bed, when I noticed the container for his retainers under the sofa. We had been looking all over for his retainers, since he had recently gotten his braces removed. I opened the container, and inside was marijuana.

Alexi and I looked at each other in disbelief.

"Now, we know what's going on with your brother," I said sadly to Alexi.

Anger, disappointment, and hurt filled my being. But at least now there was an explanation for Niko's behavior.

"I found marijuana in Niko's retainer case. How do you think we should handle this?" I asked Stelios over the phone.

"I think we should call the cops," Stelios said.

"I don't think that's necessary at this point, do you?"

As usual, we didn't agree on things. We decided to confront Niko and told him there would be no smoking pot in my house. It was illegal, and I was not going to put myself in jeopardy.

"Give me back my stuff!" Niko demanded. "I paid good money for that."

"Well, that was your poor decision," I snapped back. "It's going down the toilet."

Niko was furious, and so was I.

Don't be afraid to confront your teen if you suspect something is wrong.

More Family Meetings

It was time for more family meetings. Stelios and I decided we needed to take Niko to counseling. This was a family affair, and we all needed to go. The counselors gave us information on drugs and helped us learn to communicate better. Niko apparently had a lot of anger bottled up inside him, and this was his way of expressing it.

The family meetings did not help. Niko kept smoking, and his grades and behavior were getting progressively worse.

Everyone said cars were a big motivation at his age, and at this point, I needed any leverage I could find.

"If you go to rehab, I will buy you a car when you graduate," I offered in desperation.

Some time went by.

"Okay, Ma. My best friend, Josh, and I will go to rehab together."

"That's a great idea," I exclaimed, thankful that he had finally seen the light. Or so I thought.

Both families signed up for a rehab program, which involved classes for the parents and students, as well as counseling sessions. I was hopeful that this time, Niko was going to succeed. After months of going to classes and counseling, Niko graduated from the program.

But it turned out that nothing had really changed.

Getting off drugs is a long and difficult process. Have faith, and keep speaking words of encouragement to yourself and them.

The Last Straw

One morning in his senior year of high school, Niko descended the stairs to head off to school. I saw him put something into his jacket pocket.

"What is that in your coat pocket?" I asked suspiciously.

"None of your business," Niko snapped.

I knew it was pot—again. Niko left for school, slamming the door behind him.

Betrayed, confused, and hurt, I didn't know what to do or where to turn. Niko had promised me he would stop smoking. We had made a deal that if he stopped smoking, I would help him get a car.

I dialed the counselor's number.

"You have to call the police." The words reverberated in my ears.

How can I call the police on my own son? How can I do that?

"You are choosing life for him."

This day I call heaven and earth as witnesses against you that I have set before you life and death, blessings and curses.
Now choose life, so that you and your children may live.
(Deuteronomy 30:19-20 ESV)

The words of scripture echoed in my mind.

Every nerve in my body was on fire. I couldn't think straight. "You have to do something before he turns eighteen, or else he will go to jail and then he'll have a record," the counselor said.

Hanging up the phone, I stared into space.

As if under a spell, I picked up the phone. Slowly and deliberately, I dialed the number to Niko's school. The rest of the day was like an episode from a television drama, complete with police car chase and a visit to the hospital to evaluate Niko.

The phone rang later in the day. It was the school official.

"I regret to inform you that we have expelled Niko from school for carrying an illegal substance on school grounds."

Numb, I hung up the phone.

The Consequences

"Did you call the police on me? My own mother called the police on me! You got me expelled from school." Niko was enraged.

"You got yourself expelled, young man. All I was thinking was that you had pot in your jacket and that you lied to me about stopping. You've lied to me for the last time. I've had enough, Niko!" I yelled back, not able to hold back the tears of grief, sadness, and shame.

The right thing to do is usually the hardest thing to do.

God Is Merciful Again

Somehow, we got through another family crisis. God was merciful once again. The guidance counselor told us Niko could go to a school for kids who were having problems. We prayed and waited anxiously to see if the school would have an opening for him.

Within a few days, the school called. They had one spot available.

Niko would be in a new environment and under strict supervision and behavior guidelines. I felt like things were finally getting under control. They had been out of control for so long.

Niko finished his classes. In order to graduate, he had to get at least a C average or better and pass health class, which he had already failed twice.

"Don't worry, Ma. I've got it under control," Niko assured me. He thought he had it covered. He must have picked up that phrase from his brother.

The day came when it was time to review his grades. Unfortunately, Niko had forgotten to take into consideration a small technicality: his failing grades from the first half of the year. As the administrator reviewed his grades, we both sat there with somber looks on our faces.

"Congratulations, Niko. You will be able to graduate with your class in June."

A wave of relief washed over Niko's face. Somehow, he had managed to achieve a C average. It was a miracle.

"Congratulations, Niko. You did it," I told him. But what I meant, and what Niko knew, was that *we* did it.

Mother and son hugged each other. It was a bittersweet moment, but we had won the battle.

Hang tough with your kids. They need you to be tough for them when they can't be for themselves.

The Aftermath

Years passed, and Niko was unable to forgive me for calling the police about the marijuana. A root of bitterness festered inside him, and we grew further and further apart. He refused to kiss me or let me kiss him or even get close to him. It was heartbreaking for me. Unable to understand why I had done what I did, Niko refused to accept that I did it out of love. I, too, had my doubts that I had done the right thing, but one day I had enough.

"I am not going to discuss this topic anymore. You won't understand what I did until you have children of your own," I told Niko. I was tired of defending myself.

"If I hadn't called the police, you would never have graduated from high school at the rate you were going. You were headed straight for failure, and you ought to thank God that He gave me the strength and the courage to do what I did. I sure hope you don't have to go through this with your kids."

From that day on, the realization of the truth of the matter melted Niko's hard heart, and his attitude toward me began to soften. Slowly, we became closer. The son I had known and loved as a child was slowly coming back to me. Niko smoked on and off again for a few more years, but one day, I heard an amazing comment.

"It's been six months since I've smoked, Ma."

"Really? That's wonderful news, Niko. You must be very proud of yourself."

Step to Faith: Do the right thing. It always yields right results.

The LORD rewards every man for his righteousness and his faithfulness.
(1 Samuel 26:23 ESV)

Divorce is a very painful experience for children, no matter their age. It takes years to heal the emotional wounds, and kids try to dull the pain in any way they can, often with alcohol and drugs. I had to come to a point where I put my child into God's hands, trusting that He would heal Niko in His own time, just as He was healing me. God is gracious and merciful. He sees our pain and counts every tear we shed.

It was time: time for me to stop fighting Niko's battles and move on with my life, time for Niko to learn to trust his heavenly Father, and time for me to face my deepest fears.

Step to Faith: Remember who is on my side.

The battle is not yours, but the Lord's. (2 Chron 20:15)

CHAPTER 11

Face Your Fears

So what do you do after you've been married for so many years and suddenly find yourself single again? You get yourself in the best possible shape you can, find something you like to do, and get out there and start having some fun. Dating requires the courage to face our fears and insecurities. It is also an opportunity to learn what we want in our lives and what we will not tolerate.

Reentering the Dating Scene

"Would you like to dance?" asked an attractive dark-haired guy as he smiled at me.

"Sure would," I said, smiling back.

I had decided to get back into dancing. It was a safe enough location, and there was no alcohol, so I felt comfortable going by myself.

Peter turned out to be a good swing dancer. He was funny, talkative, and we hit it off right away. He started calling to ask if I needed a ride to the dances.

That's a good approach. No pressure, and we get to talk on the way there.

Peter was Catholic, Spanish, good-looking, and had a mustache, just like my father, interestingly enough. He was very sociable and could talk to anyone about anything. I liked that about him.

Mom liked him, because he had good teeth and a nice smile. For some reason, she was always inspecting my dates' teeth. She must have assumed that the family had money or something if they had good teeth.

Although he was Catholic and very involved with his parish, we agreed to alternate churches on the weekends. The Catholic church was a lot like the Greek church, and I much preferred the services at my new church.

Good teeth aside, there was a problem. Peter couldn't hold a steady job.

"Who does that remind you of?" Mom would ask.

It didn't seem to bother him at all, but it certainly bothered me. I was not going to get into a relationship where I was supporting a man who couldn't hold a job—like my mother had done.

One time, Peter asked me to help him with his résumé.

"Sure, I'd love to help you with it. I'm pretty good with résumés."

His was four pages long.

"How come you've had so many jobs?" I asked him. He had some explanation or excuse about every boss or company. It was never his fault. Something deep inside me quivered, as I remembered my father and the many jobs he had. It was the same story with my father: never his fault.

Red flag!

After dating for about fourteen months, things weren't going well between the two of us. Here I was, raising two small boys, working full time, and taking care of a house and a car. And all he did was complain about never having enough time with me and ask why I was so tired on the weekends. *Hello!*

Well, you'd be tired, too. That is, if you had a job and were raising two kids all by yourself.

I decided he was too needy. I was feeling very pressured, so I told him I needed to take a break. That was the end of that—for about ten years.

Missionary Dating

The next guy I dated was Jewish. His name was Jacob. He was an accountant and a much better dancer. I met him at the swing dance, as well. It was a real struggle at the beginning, about whether I should date him, since I was a born-again Christian and he was

Jewish. My church had a strong objection to dating "unbelievers," but I rationalized my feelings, thinking that perhaps God was using me to convert him. Besides, I was lonely, and he was a good dancer.

After several months of dating, I learned that dating with the intent to convert the other person is known as "missionary dating" and is to be avoided at all costs. Everything I read said to let God do the converting and that I was not "Holy Ghost Junior." Nor is it a good idea to get into a relationship with someone because you are lonely. But people do it all the time, and I was no exception.

Our relationship lasted for about five years, off and on. We were very serious about each other and spoke of marriage. We both loved dancing together, and everyone told us what a good couple we made. The situation was coming to a head, and I knew that I would soon have to make a choice.

One night at dinner, I couldn't hold it in any longer.

"I have realized that my relationship to God is the most important thing in my life. I cannot marry you," I said.

Jacob's face dropped like a heavy weight. His expression went from joyful expectation to disappointed sadness. He was devastated and heartbroken, and so was I.

Somehow, we couldn't seem to let go of each other. That's what happens when you still love someone. Although we had a lot in common, the differences in our faith were a major obstacle to overcome.

"I have a friend who is a Messianic Jewish rabbi," an acquaintance at work told me. A Messianic Jew is a Jew who believes in Jesus as the Messiah. "Why don't you make an appointment to see him, and see what he has to say?"

So we did.

Jacob and the rabbi became very close. The rabbi had been an accountant, and they had much in common to talk about. Jacob began to read the Bible and eventually came to believe that Jesus is indeed the Messiah. Nevertheless, there were still other issues in our relationship.

Jacob had a sarcastic sense of humor and was critical of me. This reminded me of my father's sarcasm and critical spirit, and I didn't like it one bit. For example, I liked to run and participated in races for charity. He constantly berated me for running, telling me I was going to hurt myself and that I'd never be able to dance when I got older. I was also afraid to tell him I was trying something new for fear of his judgment and disapproval. During tax season, he would get stressed, and these traits would come out even more.

Jacob also tended to see the negative side of things. When I would get down in the dumps, he would get right down with me. What good was that? I needed someone who would lift me up when I was down.

> *If one falls down, the other is there to lift him up.* (Eccl 4:10)

Five years and many migraines later, I realized it wasn't working out between us. I was unable to envision a future together. I still remember Jacob's parting words to me, "I understand you, but I don't accept you." With those words, I should have realized what my problem was, but I didn't until many years later.

Well, isn't that a lovely thing to say.

After several months of being apart, I received a phone call.

"We have 80 percent that's good and 20 percent that isn't. I want to work on the 20 percent," Jacob said.

I agreed to try again, but things still did not work out. The 20 percent was too much to overcome.

We remained friends, and as time went by, we were able to dance with each other again on the dance floor. We both knew we had given it our best shot and that it was time to move on, with no bitter feelings.

When a relationship ends, ask yourself what you need to learn from it.

One Sunday morning several years later, I was warming up for a race for charity.

I recognize those legs.

I walked over to see if I knew the man. Jacob turned around and smiled at me.

"What in the world are you doing here?" I asked incredulously. "The last place I would have ever expected to see you was at a race."

"I'm warming up," he said. "I'd like you to meet someone."

Jacob introduced me to his fiancée, an avid runner.

Well, God certainly has a sense of humor, that's for sure.

"I've heard so much about you," she said. "You did a really good job of training him."

We both chuckled at the comment, and I wished them both well in their marriage. Jacob had softened up after all, proving to me that people can change. I was so happy for him that he had found someone. Everybody deserves to be happy, and because two people don't see eye to eye on things doesn't mean they are not both good people.

The Atheist

Then there was the atheist. Michael was the best dancer of them all. He was kind and gentle; I liked that about him. We both knew there were major differences between us. He smoked and didn't believe in God, but we were both very lonely. We started going out as "friends," and I was very happy to have someone to dance with, as well as someone to talk to.

"Are you going to waltz night?" Michael asked me one night, referring to a gala evening our dance facility was hosting.

"I was thinking about it," I answered, waiting to see what he would say next.

"Would you like to be my guest?" he asked.

"I would love to," I replied.

How exciting! I'm looking forward to getting all dressed up, and now I even have an escort. Thank you, Lord!

Michael was beaming from ear to ear when he arrived at my door to pick me up. He wore a white tuxedo jacket and bow tie. My white dress matched his jacket, and we made a handsome couple.

"You look lovely," he said sweetly as he helped me put on my coat. I felt like Eliza Doolittle, from the movie *My Fair Lady,* going to the ball.

It was an enchanting evening. As Michael guided us smoothly around the dance floor, we were in our own little world. There is something magical about dancing that makes you forget all your cares, and that night, the spark of romance ignited between us.

Michael was a kind soul, quiet, and scholarly. He liked to read and was an experienced tennis player, who gave me good advice. After a year of dating, the difference in our beliefs was becoming more and more evident. He refused to come to church with me, even during the holidays, and this bothered me tremendously. The tension was mounting in the relationship.

I had just parked the car after a nice day of shopping together, and Michael turned to me and said, "There's something I need to say to you."

Oh my, here it comes.

Michael went on to say that he thought it was better if we stopped seeing each other. I didn't understand at the time, but later I decided that perhaps it was an indirect way of saying he couldn't deal with our religious differences. Although I felt sad at the loss, I was glad that he had the courage to end the relationship so I didn't have to.

We remained friends and continued to dance with each other from time to time when we'd meet on the dance floor.

One evening as we were dancing, Michael confided, "I think I let my ego get the best of me."

I just smiled and said, "It happens." I had let the relationship go and realized that it was for the best.

The poor man eventually got cancer and passed away, but we remained friends, and that's what really matters when a relationship ends. Michael knew he always had a friend in me.

Sex or God

Then there was Freddie—the tallest guy I ever dated. He was six feet four, and I felt safe with Freddie. We met on one of those Internet dating sites. There was a strong physical attraction between us. We could be together, not say a word, and still feel comfortable. I did suspect at times that he drank a bit more than I was comfortable with, but the main problem was that he wanted to have sex before marriage. I wanted to follow God's guidelines, which protect the sanctity of sex by preserving it for the marriage relationship. Freddie felt that our relationship would suffer if the physical piece was missing, and I felt that our relationship would suffer if we disobeyed God.

One afternoon, I received an e-mail from Freddie.

"I have been agonizing about our relationship," the e-mail said. "I understand how important your beliefs are to you and I am very conflicted. I don't want to cause you any pain, and I think it is best if we stop seeing each other."

I was shocked.

I had no idea that sex was so important to him that he would throw away the chance for a great relationship just like that. It wouldn't be great in his eyes if there were no sex, and it wouldn't be great in my eyes if there were no God.

Resolved to stay pure and true to myself and to God, I replied to his e-mail. "Dear Freddie, I understand your feelings completely, and although I am saddened that you choose to discontinue our relationship, I respect your decision. As for me, I am going to wait to find a man who will value this in me, and I am not going to allow my passions to control me." Slowly, Freddie faded from my consciousness and I moved on. I learned another painful lesson about who I was and what was important to me.

Step to Faith: Stay pure.

It is God's will that you should be sanctified: that you should avoid sexual immorality; that each of you should learn to control your own body in a way that is holy and honorable, not in passionate lust like the pagans, who do not know God. (1 Thessalonians 4:3-5)

Christian Dating

By now, as a practicing Christian woman, I realized that I needed to look for a Christian man who held the same values I did. It was with much sadness that I decided to give up looking for a partner in life on the dance floor. Being Christian became number one on my priority list, and being a good dancer fell out of the top ten.

I tried to not be too hard on myself for taking so long to come to this realization, but sometimes it is hard to give up something you love as much as I did dancing.

> *"Do not judge others, and you will not be judged."* (Matt 7:21 NLT)

Willing to Work

It was time to meet some Christian men, so I began to participate in the singles events sponsored by the church I was attending at the time. There were several nice Christian guys available, but each had his own issues.

Some were afraid of commitment. Others were still living with their mothers and could not hold a steady job. Some were too shy to even ask a woman out on a date.

One guy had potential. He had a good job, owned his own home, and was a practicing Christian. But he would have outbursts of anger when we were together. These outbursts would upset me and remind me of my father.

"I've worked very hard on my temper," he stated firmly.

"Well, I'm willing to work on the issues in our relationship," I said to him.

"If it is going to be this much work, I'd rather not," he said and walked away.

Well, that is certainly your choice. Guess you're not the one then.

We remained friends and would meet at lunch from time to time to chat and catch up with each other. He was a nice guy, but the time for a relationship between us had past.

Top Ten Must-Haves

Lord, am I being too particular?

Just as I made you, I made someone to go with you. Trust me.

It was July, and I decided to attend a Christian Singles Conference in the area. The guest speaker was Dr. Neil Clark Warren, a Christian author who had written several books on relationships, including the best seller *Date or Soul Mate.* He was also the promoter of a new Internet dating service. His theory was to make a list of the ten most important attributes that you want in a partner, as well as a list of the ten most undesirable traits, and look for someone who had each of those desired traits and none of the undesired traits. Every trait that was missing from your list of top ten must-haves would be a source of conflict and tension in your relationship.

I think I must have made my list about a million times, each time revising it as my vision of my partner became clearer and clearer in my mind.

My mother said I was being, "too particular," probably because I was holding out for a Christian man. But I didn't agree with her. Having a decent job and being willing to work through conflicts were nonnegotiable as far as I was concerned. I knew what was important to me, and as the country song by Sugarland says, "I ain't settlin'."[1]

What About Rob?

"I want to do something different this year to celebrate my birthday," I said to my girlfriend.

"Like what?" she asked.

"I've always wanted to try country line dancing. How about we try country line dancing?"

"Whatever you want," she replied. "It's your birthday."

It was exciting to have something fun and different to look forward to on my birthday.

I'll wear the boots I bought in Texas and my black leather jacket with the fringe trim.

It was a Friday night in early November, and we invited some friends to join us at a country-western dance bar and restaurant. One of my other girlfriends had been trying to get me to go there for years, but I had never mustered up the courage to go.

The band was playing, and I was enjoying the music, when I noticed a handsome man in a cowboy hat approaching our table.

I wonder if he is coming over to ask me to dance.

Sure enough, he approached our table, politely extended his hand to me. "May I have this dance?" he asked.

His name was Rob. He always wore a cowboy hat, jeans, and boots. He was the first cowboy-type I had ever met, and I was very attracted to him. I loved watching him do the line dances, and I melted every time he flashed his boyish smile.

The band played a slow dance, and Rob asked me to dance. I was very particular about with whom I slow danced, but I decided to accept. As he drew me close to him, I felt my body tingle with electricity.

I wonder if he feels this, too?

He must have, because as soon as the song was over, he asked me if I would like to go out to dinner with him sometime. I paused and immediately sent up a prayer to God, asking for direction. Having previously decided I was not going to date anyone from the dance venue again—and particularly from this place, as it was also a bar—I was not inclined to say yes.

Rob waited for my answer.

I waited for God to answer.

Give him a chance.

What's that, Lord?

Give him a chance.

It was very clear what the answer was to be. I took a deep breath and replied, "Yes, I would like to go out to dinner with you."

He smiled and asked for my phone number.

This was a Friday night. The next morning, at 9:45, my phone rang. It was Rob, wanting to know if I had plans for the evening.

He sure doesn't waste any time, does he?

Our First Date

Since we lived on the opposite sides of town, we agreed we would meet at the country dance place and then drive together to dinner. He wanted to take me to Annapolis, since he was familiar with the restaurants there. Annapolis was a quaint town on the water that bustled with shops and cozy restaurants. The conversation flowed as we drove.

I wonder if he's a Christian.

As we pulled into a parking space, Rob suddenly started talking about religion and what church he attended. It was uncanny: almost as if he were reading my mind. My antennae went up immediately.

Wow, that was curious. Wonder what prompted him to bring that up.

Rob took me to a very nice restaurant in town. As dinner was served, Rob looked at me and asked, "Would you mind if I said grace?"

"Please do," I replied, trying not to show my complete surprise. It was a rare experience for one of my dates to offer to say grace.

Thank you, Lord.

Rob called every night for the first two months. Things were going great. We went to dinner and enjoyed dancing together. He even came to church with me on Sundays. I couldn't believe it; he was everything I had been looking for. Or so I thought.

While on vacation in Texas, visiting my parents over the Christmas holiday, all I did was talk about Rob.

"Well, it's obvious you really like this guy," my parents commented.

There would be roses on my car seat when he opened the door for me and cards for no special reason except to say that he missed me. Rob was very romantic and knew how to charm a woman. It was like a dream.

This is too good to be true.

Unfortunately, it wasn't long before the issues began to arise between us. I noticed Rob had quite a few female friends at the dance hall who weren't very receptive to me at all.

"She's an old friend," he'd say.

He also always had a beer in his hand when we went out dancing.

"Your eyes look glassy," I would say to him.

"I'm tired. I've had a long day at work," was his pat response.

I began to wonder about his drinking habits.

After the holidays were over, things seemed to take a turn for the worse. The communication began to disintegrate. It was as if Rob had stopped trying.

By Valentine's Day, I knew it was over, when he made plans to see his horse trainer and forgot we had agreed to go to dinner at a comedy show.

It was hard for me to let go. I had fallen hard for Rob, and as usual, I thought that we could work things out if we both wanted.

"I don't do conflict," Rob stated one day while we were having lunch.

You don't do conflict? What does that mean?

Here was another man who didn't want to put the effort into a relationship to make it work. I was devastated.

We can work this out. I know we can work this out.

But it takes two to tango or two-step, and Rob wasn't interested in working it out.

It took me over a year to get over Rob but the Lord had something else for me to do to keep me busy which needed my full and undivided attention. It was time for a major lesson in faith and God was about to speak.

Step to Faith: Face my fears, and use my head.

For God has not given us the spirit of fear;
but of power, and of love, and of a sound mind.
(2 Timothy 1:7 NKJV)

CHAPTER 12

Learn to Listen

God is still speaking to us. The question to ask is, "Am I listening?" When God tells me to do something, usually it's in the form of a command, such as, "Go" or "Stop." It's usually pretty clear. Although it's not always easy to do what God tells me to do, I want God's best and am willing to do whatever He asks of me to get it. In the end, obedience always brings blessings.

An Ad in the Paper

One Sunday afternoon in June, I stopped at Dunkin' Donuts for a bite to eat after church. The smell of freshly baked donuts enticed me to buy some. As I waited in line, I saw a stack of Sunday papers for sale.

Buy a newspaper.

I don't usually buy the newspaper, because I don't normally have time to read it, but something told me to buy one. I've learned to listen to that inner voice.

"I'll take an egg sandwich on an English muffin, a small Dunkaccino, and this newspaper."

It was so nice to sit down, relax after church on a Sunday morning, and actually have time to read the newspaper. Sipping my hot chocolate coffee drink, I began leafing through the paper, when an ad for some new condominiums caught my eye. They were recently built and not too far from where I lived.

These look really nice, but I probably can't afford anything in that area.

The condos were located in an upscale part of town a few minutes north, so I flipped the page and didn't give the idea any more thought.

The Voice

Several weeks passed.

I think I'll remodel my dining room. It could use a face-lift.

Having just returned from a vacation in Scottsdale, Arizona, where I had fallen in love with the colors of the area, I decided on a Southwest theme. The walls would be a bright shade of coral, and the ceiling a turquoise blue reminiscent of the skies of Arizona.

It was a quiet Sunday afternoon in July, and I was hard at work, painting the walls of my dining room. My hand was raised midair, paintbrush in hand, when I heard a voice—not an audible voice, mind you, but a voice nonetheless.

Go see the condo.

I paused.

Go see the condo.

There it was again.

Over the years, I have learned to listen to that still, small voice. Obediently, I put down the paintbrush right there and then.

Step to Faith: Listen for God's still, small voice by turning off the television, radio, cell phone, and computer.

And behold, the LORD passed by, and a great and strong wind tore into the mountains and broke the rocks in pieces before the LORD, but the LORD was not in the wind; and after the wind an earthquake, but the LORD was not in the earthquake; and after the earthquake a fire, but the LORD was not in the fire; and after the fire a still small voice.

(1 Kings 19:11-12 ESV)

Why not? I have the time; I might as well go see it.

After quickly changing clothes, I phoned the complex to make sure they were open. "We're open till six p.m.," the woman said over the phone.

Plenty of time.

Falling in Love

Filled with excitement, I jumped into my car and headed north.

As I drove up the long driveway, I smiled, as I noticed the lovely landscaping.

Nice curb appeal.

The saleswoman greeted me with a cheery smile and began to show me around the property. There was a gym, a movie theater, a café, an outdoor pool, and tennis courts.

Wow, everything I ever wanted is right here.

I was falling in love with the place.

The Perfect Fit

The next day was Monday. I told my son Niko and a close girlfriend about the place. They could sense the excitement in my voice and wanted to see it right away. The three of us drove up after work.

"This is you," Karen said as she surveyed the place.

"How much is it?" Niko queried: practical, like his mom.

"A lot," I answered.

I pondered whether I wanted to part with my townhome, particularly as I had spent so much time and energy painstakingly remodeling my kitchen just a few years ago.

Then I noticed the countertops in the kitchen.

"Look, you two, these countertops are the exact same kind I put in my kitchen."

Wow, what a coincidence. What are the chances of this?

As I contemplated this coincidence, I heard the voice.

You're not losing your kitchen. I'm giving you a better one.

Tears came to my eyes. It seemed the Lord had handpicked this place just for me.

God's Best

Now, I have to tell you that I was very concerned. I wasn't sure whether the voice I was hearing was my own selfish flesh or if God really was speaking to me. I wanted so much to do God's will and be obedient.

I prayed fervently.

One day, I remembered the Old Testament story of how God had spoken to Abraham and told him to leave Egypt to go to the Promised Land. I had always wondered how Abraham knew it was God's voice speaking to him.

"I am going to step out in faith and believe that if this is God's will for me, the doors will open," I shared with another Christian friend.

"Sounds like a good plan to me," she agreed.

A sense of peace replaced my worry.

I decided to sign the contract.

What a momentous day. Another adventure in trusting God had just begun.

Step to Faith: Be courageous and take the first step.

The Lord directs the steps of the godly. (Psalms 37:23 NLT)

Big Decisions

I had sixty days to come up with the money for the down payment and still wasn't completely sure this was the right move for me. Isn't that typical of human nature—to doubt? On top of the stress of the house search, Niko was acting out again. He had graduated from high school, barely, but showed no interest in going to college or getting a job. Day after day, I would come home from work to find him lying on the sofa, asleep.

"What have you done today, Niko?" I'd ask, trying to keep my composure.

"Not much," was his typical reply. I didn't know if he was drinking or back to using marijuana, but the sight of him lying on the sofa reminded me of my father, and I didn't like it one bit. Niko had always threatened to move out as soon as he turned eighteen, but now that the time had come, he wasn't making any effort.

One day, I was at the end of my patience and decided it was time to lay down the law.

"I'm selling the house, and if you want to move in with me, you had better get your act together. Either you get a job, enroll in college, or else you can find your own place to stay. You have six months."

Tough love is hard to do, but it's even harder not to do it and then live with the consequences.

Something About New

Maybe I should look around some and see what else is available before I make this decision.

I hired a real estate agent and had him find me some units for sale in the area.

He found me a penthouse unit located in the heart of town. It had hardwood floors and a gas oven, like I wanted, but it was older, and both the kitchen and the bathroom needed remodeling. Having already gone through the pain of remodeling a bathroom and a kitchen in my townhome, I didn't want any parts of that.

The next unit he found was less expensive, but it didn't have a garage, a swimming pool, or tennis courts. I wanted to improve my living situation, didn't I?

Do I still want to scrape the ice off the car windows on cold winter mornings? No, I do not.

At work one day, I shared my qualms with a good friend.

"Well, there is something to be said about *new*," she said. "And besides, you've talked about wanting a condo for years."

"You're right, I have been, haven't I? You may be right. I've never lived in a new home before."

It was as if the Lord was giving me every opportunity to find or, more likely, to realize exactly what I wanted. It took some time to believe He had already given me his best.

If you then, who are evil, know how to give good gifts to your children, how much more will your Father who is in heaven give good things to those who ask him! (Matt 7:11 NIV)

Sell or Rent

Finally, I made the decision to stay with the first condo, which meant it was time to put my townhome on the market. The question was whether to sell or rent it out. I called my old friend Jacob, the accountant, who owned rental properties himself.

"The question boils down to this: do you want to be a landlord?" he said in a businesslike tone.

Well, that certainly puts it in perspective.

I did some research by checking with several mortgage and property management companies. It seemed that either selling it or renting it would be lucrative.

I was in bed that night when I heard the voice again. This time, it was only one word.

Unencumbered.

I knew it was God speaking to me. He didn't want me to have the burden of dealing with renters and maintenance. That's what He was trying to free me from. A peace came over me about selling the house, and I got up and went outside to put the "For Sale" sign out on the porch.

Guidance

Before I went to bed that evening, I said a prayer, asking God for guidance on whether to use a realtor. The next day was Saturday. I was standing on the front porch of my townhome, pondering the question, when a woman walked up and asked about my house. I invited her in, and we began to chat. I told her my dilemma.

"You're a Christian, aren't you?" she asked.

"Well, yes I am," I said, a bit taken aback.

How did she know?

"So am I, honey, and I think the Lord sent me here to tell you that you don't need a real estate agent. I've sold many properties myself, and these homes are selling like hotcakes. All you need is a good lawyer to write up the contract. Here's the name of the guy I use; he's great," she said, scribbling a name on a piece of paper.

I couldn't believe it and stood there, shaking my head in amazement.

Another prayer answered. Thank you, Lord.

Next was the decision about the price. The homes in the area were going for $185,000. The mortgage broker with whom I was working suggested $185,000 as well. For some reason, the figure $200,000 kept popping into my mind.

I was discussing this issue with another Christian friend of mine, and without me saying a word about the price, she said, "Ask for $200,000."

Now, where did she get that figure? Must be confirmation from the Lord.

The next day was Sunday. As soon as I returned home from church, hoards of people started streaming in my front door. The sign was doing its job. A real estate friend had advised me to use the figure $199,900 instead of $200,000 when asked the price of the house. It was a sales tactic used to make the price more appealing.

"How much are you asking," one potential buyer queried.

As instructed, I replied, "$199,900."

Two offers were made that day.

"Call me if the deal falls through," the second buyer told me.

"Will do," I promised.

The first buyer was so anxious that he called his agent to draw up a contract that same day. We made it through all the preliminaries, but the bank refused to loan him the money. I think he thought I was going to drop the price, but I did not feel led to do so. The contract expired.

Thirty days passed.

That night, I called the second buyer. He and his wife wanted to come over right away.

They were a nice couple. The man was an attorney, and he was buying the home for his daughter. I invited them in, and we sat on my sofa.

"Will you take $190,000 in cash?" the buyer offered.

I was asking $199,900. Hmmmm. What would be fair?

"Well, that's a very fine offer," I said, "but I'm asking $199,900. How about if we split the difference and make it $195,000?"

He paused a moment and then shook my hand. "It's a deal."

I was elated. After so much stress with the first buyer, I thought this one was going to be a lot easier.

Little did I know.

A Closed Door

It came time for the inspection. The buyer's real estate agent called the buyer to come over immediately.

"Uh oh, something must be wrong."

The buyer came upstairs with a sad look on his face. He was seriously concerned about some old water damage in one of the basement closets. The problem had been corrected years ago, but I never had the time to repaint the closet.

The buyer's agent had concerns over several other issues as well: the age of the roof, the electrical wiring, and a faucet in the laundry basin.

How was I going to get all these repairs fixed, let alone pay for them? Lord, please send people to help me.

One by one, friends offered to fix things. One cleaned, waterproofed, and painted the basement closet. Another, a plumber, offered to fix the faucet in the laundry basin.

Slowly but surely, all the issues were addressed but to no avail. The buyer's wife was too afraid, and the buyer wanted out of the contract. I felt the door of opportunity slam in my face.

Another thirty days went by, and to make matters worse, Niko still was not making any effort to get a job.

"Lord, are you closing the door?" I cried out as I sat on my bed that night, weeping. The pressures of everything were weighing heavily on me. "Whatever you want me to do, Lord, I will do it. If you want me to take the house off the market, I will take down the sign tonight. Just please make it clear to me what you want me to do."

Step to Faith: Trust God to make things clear.

I will instruct you and teach you in the way you should go;
I will counsel you with my eye upon you. (Ps. 32:8 ESV)

It was a Wednesday night, and I hadn't read my devotional for the day. Over the years, it has been uncanny how many times the messages have spoken to me right at my point of need.

I opened my devotional and turned to the reading for that day.

It was Genesis 12:1-12, the story of when God told Abraham to leave Egypt and to the Promised Land. I was amazed.

Lord, you heard my prayer and you answered it. Thank you, Lord, for making it so clear to me what you would have me do. I love you, Lord.

I knew in my heart it was God confirming what He wanted me to do. My mind was at peace, and I went to bed that night with a calm sense of direction.

The next morning, as I went for my morning walk, I noticed another house on the block had been sold. It was an end-of-group, just like mine.

I need to find out how much this house sold for.

That day at work, I called and asked about the particulars of the house. It sounded very much like mine.

"How much did the house sell for?" I asked the real estate agent.

The agent responded, "$199,900."

It was another sign. That was exactly the amount of money the Lord had told me to sell my house for three months ago.

Now, the pressure was really on from the saleswoman at the condo complex.

"You'd better get an agent if you want us to extend the contract," she warned.

That Sunday, I was on the phone with my stepdad, relating everything that had happened with the second contract falling through.

"Honey," he said, "you need to get a real estate agent. Why don't you call the agent who sold the house down the street?"

Just as he was saying these words, there was a knock at my front door. I asked him to hold on.

I wonder who could be knocking on my door on a Sunday morning?

"Good morning. I'm Karen with Flat Rate Realtors, and I just sold the house down the street. I saw your For Sale sign. Would you like to talk?"

Incredulous, I went back to the phone.

"You'll never guess who's at the door."

"Well, who was it?" he asked.

"The real estate agent from down the street," I answered.

"You better go talk to her," he said, chuckling.

Step to Faith: Continually ask for confirmation of my direction.

The LORD makes firm the steps of the one who delights in him; though he may stumble, he will not fall, for the LORD upholds him with his hand. (Psalms 37:23-24)

Three Days

To make a long story short, I hired that agent. They brought me two offers in three days. One of the offers was for $199,900. It was from a young man about twenty-five years old. He was trying to buy a house on his own.

"I admire your effort at taking on responsibility at such a young age. I'm going to accept your offer," I told him. Smiling, he shook my hand, and we sealed the deal.

"When would you like to move in?" I asked.

"As soon as possible."

That meant it was time to start packing. Besides the normal household items, the attic was full of stuff and old junk.

Who is going to help me empty out this place, Lord?

Fret not.

Sure enough, one morning at the gym, I was telling a girlfriend about my concerns about moving, and my old boyfriend, Peter, who also worked out at the gym, overheard our conversation.

"Would you like me to help you move?" he asked.

I couldn't believe it.

> *Ask and it will be given to you.* (Matthew 7:7)

The Showdown

The day of the big move arrived. Friends assembled at my house and everyone pitched in to get the job done.

It had been a long, busy, moving day, but the end was in sight.

"I'm taking a shower," Niko announced defiantly, obviously ready to quit for the day.

"Wait just one minute. Don't you think you ought to rephrase that question?" I could tell Niko was assuming he was moving in. The hairs on the back of my neck bristled like a porcupine's.

It had been a tiring and emotionally draining day for all of us. As Alexi and I gathered the last load into our arms, Niko went over to his car. He had waited until the very end to try to bring in his boxes.

It was time for the showdown.

My heart ached, and I didn't know if I had the courage or the strength to do what I had to do.

Lord, give me strength.

"Where do you think you're going with that stuff?"

Everyone stood still. The air was thick with tension.

"Where am I supposed to go?" Niko asked.

I paused.

Lord, give me strength.

"Niko, you've had six months to figure that out. I asked you to get a job or enroll in school, and you have done neither. I'm sure you will find a place to stay."

I turned on my heels and left my son, my baby, standing there, homeless.

It was the second-hardest thing I had to do. There's a very good reason they call it tough love.

The Lord is my strength and my shield. (Psalms 28:7)

New Homes

Major transitions in life, like moving and selling or buying a home, are very stressful. The hard part over, it was time for a whole new life for both Niko and me. As Niko figured out how to live on his own, so did I. It was the first time in my entire life that I had lived by myself, and I was very excited.

It took months to unpack all the boxes and find the right place for everything, but I enjoyed stocking my new kitchen and closets. Now, it was time for the fun part. The new year was busy with furnishing, painting, and decorating. It was a great feeling not to have to ask permission to hang something on the wall or to buy furniture.

Selling my townhome and buying my condo turned out to be one of the best decisions I've ever made: no more snow to shovel, no lawn to mow, no weeds to pull, and no trash to take outside on cold nights. The pool was only an elevator's ride away, tennis courts right on the roof, a movie theater, and a gym—everything I could possibly need or want.

Consult trusted financial experts when considering major financial investments.

"Boy, Ma, you have everything you need right here. The only time you need to go out is to get food," my oldest son remarked, smiling.

"Yes, it's like my own little piece of Heaven."

More important, Niko learned to stand on his own two feet. He got a job, enrolled in college, and for the most part, paid his own bills.

Talking about the move with Alexi reminded me of the showdown in the garage.

"Mom," Alexi said to me quite unexpectedly, "that was the bravest thing you've ever done with Niko. I am really proud of you."

As tears of the painful event welled up in my eyes, Alexi put his arms around me and gave me one of his bear hugs that I love so much.

"Thank you, honey. It was one of the most difficult things I've ever done in my life."

Other people are watching our actions and our decisions, so be strong and true to yourself—no matter what.

God Listens

Our God is an awesome God, who is concerned with every detail of our lives. He is more than willing to answer prayers and supply all our needs. In fact, He promises to do so.

> *My God shall supply all your needs according to his riches and glory in Christ Jesus.* (Philippians 4:19)

All we have to do is trust Him enough to ask. He does not want us to be overly burdened with the cares of this world.

> *Cast your cares on Him, for He cares for you.* (1 Peter 5:7)

He wants us all to live a life that is "unencumbered."

The Lord was with me every step of the way on this major transition in my life. He gave me supernatural strength to do the right thing with my home and my son. Being human, I had my doubts at times, but I trusted Him to answer and guide me, and He always did. God wants his children to move up to the high places. As He guided and directed me, He will guide and direct you if you are willing to listen and obey.

Step to Faith: Learn to recognize the voice of God.

My sheep listen to my voice; I know them, and they follow me. (John 10:27)

The Lord was indeed simplifying my life, and there was a reason why. It was time to concentrate on my healing.

CHAPTER 13

Keep the Faith

When we are longing for a dream to materialize, each year that passes seems to make our hearts heavier with disappointment. It is difficult to keep having faith, trusting, and praying, but that is what brings our dream to us. Faith that God is working on our behalf, even when we can't see any evidence at all, gives us the power to keep on believing, hoping, and praying. God is not required to give us a timetable. Much depends on our learning the lessons before us.

And whatever you ask in prayer, you will receive if you have faith.
(Matthew 21:22 ESV)

Second Chances

"I need to talk to you," my girlfriend said with a tone of urgency one night at the swing dance.

Not knowing what was going on, I followed her obediently into the ladies room.

"Well, what is it?" I asked.

Taking a deep breath, she said to me, "Why don't you give Peter a second chance? He still likes you, you know."

"What? After all these years? Are you crazy?"

"He still likes you. I think you should give him another chance. Besides, what have you got to lose?"

"I'll think about it," I told her, not feeling at all comfortable with the idea.

Some time went by, and I reconsidered my friend's suggestion.

Well, what can it hurt? The man apparently still has feelings for me after all these years, and perhaps it will help me get over Rob.

We rekindled our relationship and began dating. After a few short months, Peter surprised me.

"I have something I want to show you," he said, reaching into his pocket. He pulled out a cut ruby and placed it in my hand. "What do you think of this for an engagement ring?"

I was shocked. It was clear Peter was intent on getting married quickly. It had been over ten years since we dated, and he was acting as if it were yesterday. I certainly wasn't going to jump into anything after only a few months of dating. I had just gone through a major transition in my life, and here he was, talking about moving again and getting married. I was in no frame of mind to think about either of these. Talk about poor timing.

It didn't take long for the pressure to resume. The man hadn't changed much. He still did not have a job, and he still wanted a lot of my time. It was time to say good-bye to Peter once and for all.

It is rare for people to change much of their basic personality, so don't waste time going back to old boyfriends.

Dance Class

Now that I wasn't seeing anyone, I had time on my hands. One Saturday night, I visited a dance studio I had taught at during the disco era. The owners loved me and were very happy to see me.

"Would you consider coming back to teach for us, Ariel?" the owner asked.

I was so surprised. I asked a few questions and told him I would have to give it some thought. After giving the idea prayerful consideration, I decided it might be fun after all, since I had enjoyed it so much in the '70s.

It was to be a survivor basics ballroom class on Friday nights for six weeks. On the first night of class, twenty-two students showed up. Somewhat nervous at the size of the class, I surveyed the group. A tall, handsome gentleman stood out from the crowd.

Wow! Isn't he good looking?

After introducing myself, I asked my students to go around the room and tell me their names.

I pointed to the tall gentleman on the end and said, "Let's start with you."

His name was Noah. He was very shy and reserved. I wasn't sure for the first few weeks whether the woman he was dancing with was his girlfriend or only his partner in class. Knowing he was one of my students certainly made teaching something to which I could look forward. Each week, I hoped he would ask me to go out after the lesson. But the weeks went by, and he never did.

After teaching for about three months, I decided it was too much for me to put together a two-hour dance class, as well as the music to go with it, and teach for several hours on a Friday night after working all week at my job. On the last night of class, I explained to my students I would no longer be teaching. Somehow, the topic of exercise came up, and Noah mentioned that he took an exercise class at a studio in my area. I said I was interested in getting the name of it and offered him my e-mail address. I chuckled.

Lord, you stepped in at the very last moment.

The door was opened, and Noah began sending me e-mails.

Another First Date

"A friend of mine is having a party. Would you like to go?" Noah asked.

We had a nice time, and afterward, he asked if I would like to get a coffee. We stopped at a nearby coffee shop, where we talked and got to know each other better. I shared about my marriage and divorce. Then, it was Noah's turn. Hesitant at first, Noah slowly began to share.

"Well," he paused. "The reason I'm divorced is because I had an affair," Noah confessed, hanging his head. This should have been another red flag to me, but I didn't want to judge the guy. I'd made enough mistakes of my own.

It was apparent the guilt was still weighing heavily on him.

"We all make mistakes, Noah. As long as you have truly repented in your heart, God forgives you," I assured him.

"Thank you for being so understanding. I will never do such a thing again."

Practice forgiving—yourself, others, and God.

We started dating, and the attraction between us was electric. I resolved not to let things go too far, as I didn't want to have any regrets if things didn't work out between us. I had been down this road before.

Signs of Jealousy

"Why didn't you call me yesterday?"

"Why didn't you tell me about the bull roast?"

"Why can't you spend more time with me?"

Before long, the demons of jealousy, anger, and insecurity began to surface. Despite being so tall and attractive, Noah was very unsure of himself and emotionally dependent. It was apparent that Noah was accusing me of the same things he had done to his wife. He was projecting his fears onto me, despite the fact that I had never given him any reason to think I was untrue to him.

"I'm a working woman with a demanding job, two sons, and a lot of responsibilities," I told him.

"Well, I have as much to do as you do," he retorted.

Really? You don't have any kids, your house needs work, and you don't have any friends.

Here was another man who wanted a lot of my time. Noah was used to being with women who wanted to spend all their free time with him. I was also teaching an exercise class at the time, one night a week, to help stay in shape.

I'll stop teaching, and that will give me more time for Noah.

We tried to work things out for a few more months by going to couples counseling. All Noah wanted to do in the sessions was vent his frustrations, which got us nowhere. It was clear that Noah had issues that needed to be resolved, and the question was whether he wished to address them.

He didn't.

He broke up with me, and I was devastated. I was truly in love with Noah and thought we could work through our issues. I didn't realize these were his deep-seated problems that would take a lot of courage and effort to correct, and apparently Noah wasn't willing to put forth the effort.

I kept hoping that he would change his mind and call, and that we would get back together to try to work things out. But it never happened.

No matter how much we care for someone, we can't make the individual change; we can only change ourselves.

A Needle in a Haystack

Another year went by before I was over Noah, and I had nearly lost hope of ever meeting the man of my dreams. It seemed my life was one failed relationship after another. I still hadn't found a man who met my top ten must-haves, and it only made matters worse when potential suitors would tell me that I was, "severely narrowing my field," and that I was, "looking for a needle in a haystack," when I told them I was looking for a Christian man.

Well, maybe God doesn't want me to be married after all. I'm happy single.

I had a good life, a good job, and a nice home. My kids were grown. I had many friends and attended a great church. I decided to enjoy my life.

Another Lesson

One hot, summer afternoon, I was relaxing at the pool, enjoying the warmth of the sunshine on my lunch hour. Very few people visited the pool during the week, but I noticed a man who was there on a regular basis.

"How are you today?" the man asked as I was settling into my lounge chair.

"Just fine. Enjoying my lunch hour here at the pool."

"So am I."

Denny was quite friendly and sociable. I found out he was Catholic and went to church from time to time. The real test, however, is not so much whether or not someone goes to church, but how he behaves under pressure.

A friendship of sorts developed, and Denny asked me to have lunch. He was a casual kind of guy—no pressure—and I liked his approach. He wasn't needy or dependent, and was always ready to offer advice, listen, or lend a helping hand. It only takes a few dates to start having feelings for someone, and I found myself looking forward to seeing him at the pool. We found out we shared other interests besides the pool. Denny loved the Beatles, and so did I.

"Want to stop by my place this evening? I have a lot of Beatles music we could listen to," Denny suggested.

"I'd like that," I replied. When I arrived, Denny brought out his guitar and songbooks, and we had fun singing Beatles' songs together.

"Would you like something to drink?" Denny asked, heading to the kitchen.

"A glass of water will be fine," I replied, joining him.

As Denny reached for a glass, I noticed that the entire cabinet was full of highball glasses. There wasn't a water glass in sight.

Hmmmm, that's interesting.

Now, I was aware of my heightened sensitivity to people who drank, since my father had been an alcoholic, but I had no objection to others' drinking, and I drank wine occasionally. Not wanting to make assumptions, I started asking questions.

"How do you tell if someone has a drinking problem?" I asked some friends.

"Watch when you go out together. If it always has to be a place where there is alcohol involved that is a sure sign."

It was July, and I hosted a Fourth of July party. Denny kindly offered to help with the event. Having parties is a lot of fun, but a lot of work as well.

"I'll bring the beer," he offered. He showed up with a cooler full of beer and wine coolers and put it outside on the balcony.

Well, that was nice of him. He wanted to make sure there was alcohol at the party.

After the party, my oldest son, Alexi, remarked about how many beers Denny had downed during the evening. I had noticed Denny's eyes glaze over on more than one occasion, and this behavior was beginning to look like a red flag to me.

Patterns and Puzzles

We continued to date, and I started to take note of where Denny would take me and how much he would drink when we were together. It was always to a place where there was alcohol. Even though I enjoyed his company and he never got out of line or lost control, his drinking bothered me. I didn't know what to do about it and the issue was affecting me more than I realized.

About a week later, I was sitting at my desk at work, talking to someone on the phone.

"Kelly, I don't feel well all of a sudden. I need to talk to you later."

A blanket of dizziness covered me, and I almost fell on the floor.

Wow, something is very wrong here. I had better tell somebody.

"Could someone please call 911? I'm not feeling well at all."

The paramedics came and took me to the hospital. My body was shaking, and I was having chills. Puzzled, the doctors gave me some medicine for nausea and vertigo and sent me home after several hours.

I began to have frequent, unexplainable, dizziness episodes. I had to take time off from work, because the episodes would make me so weak, and the medicine would sedate me for hours. The doctors didn't know what the problem was. I went to see a neurologist for the first time in my life.

"You could be having migraines without the headache," she pronounced.

"Migraines without headache? I've never heard of such a thing."

Over the years, I'd had a history of migraines, but watching my diet and identifying my triggers seemed to alleviate the headaches for the most part. I didn't recall having one in several months. It was a very difficult time, being off from work and not knowing what was causing these terrible symptoms.

Subconscious Fears

Denny was supportive and even took me to the emergency room when I needed to go the next time. Although he was a kind man and cared a lot about me, I realized that my fears about his drinking were working on my subconscious. I was afraid of his drinking and more afraid to say anything to him about it. I felt that if I said something, he would feel like I was judging him. There I was again: acting codependently. I was more worried about his feelings than my own, and I didn't want to risk losing his friendship or being rejected by yet another man.

"I know what's wrong with you," Denny said to me one day, looking into my eyes. "My drinking is what's making you sick."

Softly, I whimpered in agreement, "Yes, I think that's what it is, too."

Tearfully, we decided to stop dating each other yet remain friends. It was like the blanket was lifted, and the pressure was off.

Lord, you are the great healer. Even though the doctors don't know what's wrong with me, I know you do. Please heal me.

Slowly, I began to recover, and the dizzy spells went away. It seemed my subconscious was trying to tell me not to get involved with this man because of my history with my alcoholic father. It was too much for me to deal with, and perhaps, God was protecting me in some way.

The Healing Miracle

Two months later, I was back at work, feeling better, and had planned to stop at Trader Joe's, a California-based grocery store, to pick up some items. After that, I was to meet a friend for tennis. As accidents happen, a passenger had tripped and fallen getting off the commuter train I was on, causing it to run late. When I finally got to my car, it was clear I didn't have time to get to Trader Joe's and still meet my friend on time for tennis.

Lord, what should I do?

Go to Trader Joe's.

I called my friend, and she agreed to meet me a bit later. So, off I went to Trader Joe's.

As I was getting a shopping cart, I saw a woman who looked familiar. I walked up to take a closer look to be sure it was her.

"Katherine, is that you?"

"Ariel, how are you? It's so good to see you. It's been ages."

"You know, it has been on my mind to call you for some time now. I heard you have been ill and out of work." A mutual friend had told me Katherine had been ill for quite a while.

"Oh, so you've heard about my adventures," Katherine quipped.

"Well, only that you've been out sick, and I wanted to see how you were doing. I've been out sick as well."

"Really?" Katherine exclaimed, her eyes opening wide.

As we started to commiserate on our shared experiences and frustrations with doctors and their diagnoses, the bond between us was strengthened by the similarities of it all.

"So, what did the doctors say you have?" I asked.

"Migraines without the headache, and they don't know what to do about it. I've been all over the country seeing doctors."

I stood there stunned.

How could we both have been diagnosed with the same ailment?

"That is exactly what they told me I have," I said incredulously.

"Really?" Katherine asked in amazement. "How long have you been out of work?"

"Two months. I went back to work last week. And you?"

"I'm not back to work yet," Katherine said. "I've been out for ten months."

I stared at her in unbelief.

Then I realized.

God had healed me. I trusted Him for healing, and He had healed me in two short months.

Expect miracles. God is still in business.

I could not even imagine what Katherine must have been going through for so long. My immediate thought was to pray for her, even though I wasn't sure of her beliefs.

"May I pray for you?" I offered.

"Sure," Katherine replied.

Right there in Trader Joe's, I laid hands on my friend. I put one hand on her forehead and prayed for healing from her headaches. Bravely, I ended the prayer, "In Jesus' name, amen."

Katherine looked up at me, and there were tears in her eyes.

"Thank you," she said. "Thank you very much."

We exchanged phone numbers and promised to keep in touch.

By now, I knew that with God there were no such things as coincidences. This was a divine appointment. God had work for me to do that day, and He had orchestrated the whole train situation so that I would be at the store at the exact time as my friend. God used my pain and suffering as an encouragement to someone else. And in the end, isn't that what it's all about?

> *For I am the Lord who heals you.* (Exodus 15:26)

Repeat Lesson

A year or so went by, and two friends as well as my mother suggested I try one of the Christian Internet dating services.

That's three people now who have suggested this to me recently. Maybe this is a sign from God.

I signed up for a six-month membership. Shortly before the expiration date, I received a match from a good-looking guy who lived nearby. To make a long story short, the chemistry between us was off the charts, and we began dating.

Unfortunately, he turned out to have some of the same issues Noah had: jealousy, insecurity, and emotional instability. I kept making excuses, refusing to see what everyone else saw: we were not a match. After two years of constant conflict, numerous breakups, and counseling, I realized the relationship was taking too much of a toll on me.

Lord, what am I doing wrong?

You're putting your relationships with these men above your relationship with Me.

Wow. The revelation hit me like a ton of bricks. I really was. I knew deep in my heart that this relationship was not working, but I kept trying to make it work when it wasn't meant to be.

A Humbling Revelation

After spending much time in prayer and seeking guidance and wisdom, it became clear that each of the men I had dated had one or more of my father's negative characteristics. They either couldn't keep a job; had a drinking problem; a negative, sarcastic sense of humor; were a womanizer; had jealousy, trust, or anger issues; or had some combination thereof. I was subconsciously trying to resolve the relationship with my father by attempting to "fix" my partners.

Although I kept seeing the pattern, for some reason, I was blind to the red flags when I met new men. I would rationalize their behavior, make excuses for them, and assume responsibility for their problems—the same as I had done with my ex-husband. I steeled myself into dealing with these people, thinking that I could overcome the issues. Somewhere deep down, I thought I could fix the problems if I tried hard enough. Perhaps I was even thinking, if they really loved me, they would change. What I should have done was run for the hills.

Am I trying to play God?

This revelation was humbling to say the least.

Lord, please forgive me. Have mercy.

It took a very long time to realize what I was doing. It was not my responsibility to fix other people but it was my responsibility to fix myself. It took even longer to break the habit. Codependent thinking patterns kept me focused on others instead of protecting and taking care of me.

What is Codependency?

Codependency means taking responsibility for other peoples' feelings, actions, and behavior to the neglect of one's own. I had confused caring *about* people with caring *for* people, which is both unhealthy and dysfunctional. We are each responsible for dealing with our own feelings and behavior and for making ourselves emotionally whole and healthy. But we cannot do it alone.

Regular reading of recovery literature opened my eyes to my codependent patterns and showed me areas I needed to work on. The more I read, attended share groups, and received counseling, the more I learned about how to take care of myself and deal with others.

> *If you see yourself repeating the same patterns, do yourself a favor and get good counseling.*

Codependency has many facets to it, but by educating ourselves and taking small steps of faith, we can be emotionally whole once again. It is God's will for us to be healed.

> *'But I will restore to you health and heal your wounds,' declares the Lord . . ."* (Jer 30:17 NIV)

What I Learned

There were many lessons I needed to learn about myself, codependency, and God. I was unable to say no to certain behaviors, since I was a people-pleaser. By not saying no, I was only hurting myself. Saying yes when my heart wasn't in it was being dishonest to myself, as well as the other person. It was time to stop allowing hurt and disrespect and start taking care of me.

I learned to recognize when others were trying to control or manipulate me. I also realized that I, too, had some control issues that needed to be dealt with. We may think we are in control, but when we learn to let go and let God, things go a lot smoother with much less anxiety.

God does not want us to live with anxiety. Anxiety steals our peace and joy and triggers our destructive behavior patterns. We can deal with anxiety by opening up and sharing our thoughts and fears with another person. It took me many years to learn to speak up for myself and not be so compliant when I felt uncomfortable.

Yes, this requires courage, vulnerability, and risk, but we must act in faith if we want to live peaceful lives with others. By taking small steps to communicate more, we can minimize the anxiety we feel on a daily basis, as well as protect ourselves from further pain. We may get hurt again, but we will eventually learn to be selective about who and what we allow into our lives. Unless someone demonstrates they are actively pursuing change, I need to accept them as they are or move on.

Detach in Love

It was also high time to move on from worrying about other people's issues. I needed to separate myself from their problems and give up the bad habit of offering unsolicited advice. This codependent behavior only distanced others and was certainly not helpful. People do not like to be told what to do. It implies that they are not capable enough to figure out the problem on their own. Although I saw giving advice as caring and helpful, others did not. I needed to focus on correcting my own issues and problems, and allow my loved ones to take responsibility for themselves.

We can avoid worry by detaching from others in love. We cannot change other people, and acting out of fear only distances us from those we love and those for whom we care. God is their Higher Power as well, and He will guide them in their path—the same way He is guiding us. What I didn't learn until several years later was that the "fixing" piece was only part of the problem.

The Need for Approval

Unbeknownst to my conscious mind, I was trying to get the love and approval from unavailable men that I had never received from my father. Deep inside was a little girl craving her father's love and approval. Although I knew God loved me, subconsciously, I was still trying to heal the wound of never having a loving father. Whatever man was in my life at the time, I repeated the same behaviors by giving up my needs to please and gain approval from him.

This need for approval manifested itself in various forms: from always looking to please my partner, spouse, or child over myself; to overachieving and trying to do too much; to the need for everything to be perfectly under control. Although I realized I struggled with perfectionism to some degree and had worked on being less so over the years, I never realized that the root cause of this behavior stemmed from needing approval.

Unanswered Prayer

I also learned when my prayers are not answered, it may be because I am not ready to receive what I am asking for. God knows what is truly good for us, what we can and cannot handle, and His timing is always perfect. Instead of wondering why God is taking so long, I must accept responsibility for the fact that it may be my failure to learn my lessons that is delaying God's answers.

It's Our Choice

Healing is a process that unfortunately hurts almost as much as the wounding. It involves reprogramming our thinking as well as facing our fears and losses in our lives.

But we have a choice. We can either stay in our rut continuing the same hurtful behaviors and patterns, or we can ask for God's help and strength to come to grips with our patterns and begin to respond differently. Transformation will not happen overnight, but God is patient with us, so we must be patient with ourselves.

The good news is that by choosing to heal, we allow ourselves the opportunity to grow past our old behaviors and put a stop to the hurt and pain we have suffered for so long. When we decide to change our old habits and erroneous thinking patterns, we can begin to solve problems from a new perspective. As Albert Einstein said, "No problem can be solved from the same level of consciousness that created it. You must learn to see the world anew."[1]

By changing our thoughts, we are able to change our behaviors and our responses. We no longer have to react to situations, but we can choose to respond in love for ourselves and others.

So the question to ask ourselves is, do I want to be healthy and whole, or not? The choice is up to us.

Life is an opportunity to heal our wounded souls.

No matter how deep the stain of your sins, I can take it out and make you as clean as freshly fallen snow. (Isaiah 1:18 TLB)

Step to Faith: Keep on praying.

The prayer of a righteous person is powerful and effective. (James 5:16)

Speaking of praying, there was something I had been praying about for years that was about to come true.

CHAPTER 14

God Has the Plan

"What do you mean they're selling the building?"

"Haven't you seen the newspapers yet? They're turning our building into a hotel."

"Oh my gosh. I wonder what they're going to do with us now? This is the last thing any of us ever expected."

Life doesn't always turn out the way we planned. Poor choices and unexpected losses can derail us from our intended destination. We worry about how our lives are ever going to work out when our plans don't materialize the way we had hoped. Relax, because God has the plan, and all we have to do is trust Him.

My Plan

In high school, French and Spanish came easily. Whereas other kids struggled with the grammar, pronunciation, and tenses, I struggled with science. I decided to major in foreign languages in college. My plan was to move to New York after graduation and work for the United Nations as an interpreter.

This was not to be, however, as I met my future husband while I was still in college, and we decided to marry. There went my dreams of moving to the Big Apple.

Stelios didn't want me commuting to Washington, DC, and neither did I. The only option in the Baltimore area was to find a job as a bilingual secretary, but everywhere I applied, they told me that I was overqualified.

Mom's Plan

Mom had started dating a man who was a vice president of a very large company in the area.

"Can you get Ariel at job at your company?" Mom asked her boyfriend.

"I'll see what I can do to get her in," he replied.

Soon thereafter, the company called for an interview. I was hired and began a career that was to span the next thirty plus years.

"They're going to move us to Florida," was the constant rumor. The headquarters was located in Florida, and everyone feared that the company would move us down south. No one wanted to move, but the rumors circulated year after year, like a dark cloud hanging over us, threatening to burst at any minute.

I'll cross that bridge if and when I come to it.

Worrying about things that may never happen steals your joy.

> *Do not be anxious about anything, but in every situation, by prayer and petition, with thanksgiving, present your requests to God.*
> (Philippians 4:6)

Stelios's Plan

Stelios was in the computer programming field. He had studied math and computers in college and was working as a computer science engineer for another big company in the area.

"Why don't you take some computer courses?" he suggested. "Maybe you can get into the MIS department at your company."

If I could get a job in management information services, as it was called back then, I would be in management instead of the union. I would have normal hours instead of shift work and a much better salary, not to mention my own desk.

"I took a course in college, but I don't know if I'd be any good at it."

"I'll help you," Stelios said.

I signed up for a computer course at a local college and spent my evenings in the lab or at home, pouring over thick printouts of computer programs. Programming did not come easily to me, because my mind was not trained in analytical thinking. But I persevered and got a good grade in the course.

Somewhere along the line, Stelios decided to apply for a job at my company and was hired into the department as a computer engineer. He encouraged me to try to apply for one of the management trainee positions to get into the department as well. The jobs were sparse, and I heard they didn't hire spouses in the same department.

Year after year, I applied for the computer jobs that went up on the board but never got an interview. I was about to lose hope when at last I got an interview but not the job. A few more years went by, and another opening went up on the board.

I'm going to give this one more try, and if I don't get it this time, I'm going to forget it.

I got the job.

Finally, I will have my own desk. Thank you, Lord, thank you!

After years of being a transient office clerk, it was a great feeling to come in to work every day, have my own desk, my own phone, and a place to park all my personal belongings. I was set.

If you are ready to quit knocking, God may be ready to answer the door, so don't.

Ask and it will be given to you; seek and you will find; knock and the door will be opened to you. For everyone who asks receives; the one who seeks finds; and to the one who knocks, the door will be opened.
(Matthew 7:7-8)

Management's Plan

Every company has a rumor mill, and mine was no different. It seemed anything that happened in the company would stir up the rumors of moving to Florida. At every staff meeting, someone would invariably bring up the question to upper management, who would invariably state there were no plans to move anyone at this time.

Until one day . . .

The vice president of our company showed up in Baltimore unexpectedly and announced that the company was cutting jobs to cut costs.

"We're closing Baltimore," he said. "You have a choice to either sign a separation agreement or move to Florida."

At first, everyone was shocked. Then, we got mad and decided to fight back.

We got the union involved.

We took up petitions.

We weren't going without a fight.

Relocating to Florida would mean uprooting families, severing relationships, starting all over again, making new friends, and adjusting to a strange, new city. That was fine if you were in your twenties or thirties, but most folks who worked in Baltimore were older and looking toward retirement. Moreover, rumor had it that the pressure and the politics were much more intense "down there."

Management soon realized that the Baltimore contingent wanted to stay in Baltimore. They announced a new agreement: if thirty-five employees would voluntarily leave the company by accepting a severance package, the Baltimore office would remain open.

How long will we be in Baltimore?

No one knew for sure. This was certainly a time to ask the Lord for direction.

It was an agonizing decision for many. Fears of moving to Florida caused many to consider the buyout.

"Please ask God what you should do, and listen for his voice. Each person's situation is different," I advised the folks who attended my lunchtime Bible study group.

Ask God when making life-changing decisions. Pray and then pray some more.

> *Therefore if any of you lacks wisdom, he should ask God who gives generously to all without finding fault, and it will be given to him.*
> (James 1:5)

I've always wanted to live at the beach. Maybe this is God's way of answering my request.

I chose to stay with the company and trust God for my future, whatever it held.

More people put in for the buyout. The company accepted all the offers, and it was back to business as usual for several years.

Until one day . . .

"Did you see the article in the newspaper?"

Everyone was buzzing.

What now?

"They've sold the building, and they're turning it into a hotel!"

Incredible. Now, that's something no one ever considered. What's going to happen to us now?

When you don't know what's going to happen next, relax, because God does.

God's Plan

"We have decided to offer the employees of Baltimore two options. You may either elect to work at another unspecified location in the state, or you may elect to work from home and telecommute on a full-time basis."

No one could believe the offer from management. What an unexpected turn of events. After all these years of living in fear of moving south, the company was offering us the opportunity to telecommute. It was beyond our wildest dreams and something I had prayed about for years.

The company decided to pay us $1,000 to help set up our home offices, plus a monthly stipend to help defray the costs of Internet service. They would also provide a company phone, so we would not incur long distance phone charges. What more could one ask?

This is a miracle—an absolute miracle! Of course, I am going to choose to telecommute!

No more fighting rush hour traffic, no more getting up before dawn to exercise before work, no more having to get all dressed up and put on makeup. Life was definitely going to be simpler, and my prayer of working from home had been answered at long last.

God has a plan for your life that sometimes takes years to be revealed.

God is awesome. He rewarded me for all my years of service, perseverance, and trust.

One by one, He was removing the hindrances and stresses in my life and transporting me to a place of serenity, freedom, and joy.

Step to Faith: Know that God is in control, and He has the plan.

"For I know the plans I have for you," declares the Lord, "plans to prosper you and not to harm you, plans to give you a hope and a future."
(Jeremiah 29:11)

CHAPTER 15

Be Set Free

Have you ever felt completely free?

I mean really free—from guilt, shame, and fear, from the burdens and bondages of debt, an unhappy marriage, emotional baggage, even yard work? Have you ever felt so free that you want to dance and jump for joy like you did as a child?

What a great feeling. Free is how God wants us to feel every single day. I was finally free from unhealthy thinking patterns, free to make my own choices and decisions, and best of all, free to be myself.

True freedom has to do with the human spirit—
it is freedom to be who we really are[1]

What is sad is that most of us don't even realize that we are not free. We start off as children, being carefree and living in the moment. But then as we grow up, we learn erroneous thinking patterns, make poor choices, and life happens. We saddle ourselves with all kinds of responsibilities, debts, and obligations and then flop into bed at night, exhausted from the daily grind. We become addicted to fill a void or a need in our lives. Our addiction could be our job, overeating, abusing a substance, overachieving, seeking approval, or people-pleasing, to name a few. In fact, anything we do to excess may be an addiction.

But this is not the kind of life God intended for us. Jesus is the only one who can fill the void in our lives. He came to set us free from all these things so we can fly like eagles.

> *So if the Son sets you free, you will be free indeed.* (John 8:36)

Free from My Past

As I sat in the huge auditorium during a Christian concert, the words of the worship leader resonated in my soul.

"You are free in Christ. Be who God created you to be, and don't be ashamed of yourself."

The band broke out in song, and I was on my feet.

"I am free to dance, I am free to run, I am free, I am free."

Jumping and dancing joyfully to the music, my soul felt liberated.

This is how it feels to be free.

It was incredible. After so many years of taking on too many responsibilities, trying so hard to please others, and being in emotionally damaging relationships, I was no longer in bondage to anything or anyone. I was free from an abusive and joyless marriage and from many of my old fears and beliefs. My emotions were under better control, and, consequently, so were my weight and finances.

At last, I had found my voice, and it was time to be heard. As my faith increased, so did my ability to speak up for myself. I practiced expressing my feelings and my fears, and standing up for what I believed was right. My past was behind me, and I was not about to let anyone take me back there again. Now it was time to choose my future.

Free to Choose

Having faith helped me to realize that I can make good choices, and this had a huge impact on my outlook on life. I learned to make choices that were in alignment with my values and priorities and not someone else's. Each conscious choice I made helped me become a little more empowered and strengthened my faith in myself and in God.

Just because someone at the office brought in donuts didn't mean I had to eat one. Just because everyone else was staying late at the nightclub or the dance didn't mean I had to stay late as well. I learned that making the right choice for me was far more important than following the crowd or caring what other people might think. Small daily choices—such as what to eat and when, when to rise and when to go to bed, and whether I would exercise—made me feel good about myself. Success in these choices gave me the faith and courage to make bigger and more important decisions. It was a matter of taking responsibility for my life.

But the greatest revelation was that I could choose my attitude. Despite my circumstances, I can choose to free my mind of negative thoughts. Viktor Frankl was a neurologist and psychiatrist. He was also a Holocaust survivor. While an inmate in a concentration camp in Auschwitz, Frankl pondered the meaning of life. In his book *Man's Search for Meaning,* Frankl states:

> Everything can be taken from a man but . . . the last of the human freedoms—to choose one's attitude in any given set of circumstances, to choose one's own way.[2]

This concept is so empowering. Thoughts were things I could control. I did not have to dwell on anxiety-provoking fearful thoughts. I could choose to think about something good. My favorite Scripture verse became:

> *Fix your thoughts on what is true, and honorable, and right, and pure, and lovely, and admirable. Think about things that are excellent and worthy of praise.*
> (Philippians 4:8 NLT)

Now that I no longer had the need to please anyone or gain anyone's approval, I realized it was time to slow down the hectic pace of my life.

Free from Busyness

When I was so busy raising my sons, I didn't have much alone time. I was constantly on the go, doing this and that. I would rush from one activity to the next, trying to fit it all in. There was so much to do and no one to help me. Now that my sons were grown and I was living on my own, I realized that the need to live at such a frantic pace was gone.

It was time to slow down and relax: time to enjoy spending time with myself and God.

Many people don't like to be by themselves. They always have to have someone around, somewhere to go, or something to do. The television or radio is their constant companion. These days, many people walk around with an iPod attached to their ear, or they're texting away on their cell phone at a nonstop pace.

Now, please don't misunderstand. I'm not saying there's anything wrong with any of these gadgets or keeping in touch with others. What I am saying, though, is that when we listen to the world more than we listen to that still, small voice, we pay a huge price and miss hearing from God, and consequently, His great blessings.

Instead of rushing off to the gym first thing on Saturday, I use the quiet hours of the morning to nourish my spirit. It is so relaxing to sit outside on my balcony, take in the view, and enjoy the sounds of the birds chirping. It is a perfect time to read my Bible, write in my journal, and connect with God.

Be still and know that I am God. (Psalms 46:10)

After a hectic week at work, I treasure the precious morning hours and appreciate not having to be somewhere at a certain time. When I am quiet, I can hear His voice more clearly. In fact, I guard my times with Him as closely as I do time with my sons. As parents love spending time with their children, so our Heavenly Father loves when we make time to be with Him, dwell in his presence, and listen for His voice. When we spend time with Him, we realize we are never truly alone, because He is always with us.

> *Then when you call, the Lord will answer; and He will say, here I am.*
> (Isaiah 58:9)

Free to Commit

Faith is about learning to commit. It is having the confidence that God will see you through whatever decision you make. Faith is the fuel that fires up our engine. Without it, we become inert and idle through life. We succumb to fear and, like a car with a dead battery, stop moving forward on our journey.

> *What good is it, my brothers and sisters, if someone claims to have faith but has no deeds? Can such faith save them? Suppose a brother or a sister is without clothes and daily food. If one of you says to them, "Go in peace; keep warm and well fed," but does nothing about their physical needs, what good is it? In the same way, faith by itself, if it is not accompanied by action, is dead.*
> (James 2:14-16 NIV)

To commit is to be loyal to something or someone. It could be a commitment to ourselves to reach a personal goal, to a spouse, a child, a job, or a church. It means acting on my values instead of my feelings.

Commitment also means agreeing to do something in the future. It means keeping my word and my promises. Keeping our commitments helps us become people of integrity and honor. It helps us develop character and self-respect.

The opposite of faith is fear, an invisible enemy that lurks deep within the murky waters of our subconscious mind. Fear affects how we think, how we act, and the choices we make. Until we shine the light of faith and truth on our fears, we will remain in bondage to them and be unable to make and keep commitments in order to move forward in life.

Having been in a controlling marriage, gone through a painful divorce, and endured numerous unhealthy relationships, I had developed a fear of commitment. I did not want anyone to control me again or limit my newfound freedom. But what I learned was that by making conscious choices within my value system, I could make and keep commitments that enabled me to live a full and abundant life.

Learning to trust God enables us to make and keep commitments.

It's time to join the church.

It was a bit scary to hear this, to tell you the truth.

Am I ready to join the church? What am I getting myself into?

Until then, I wasn't a committed member of any church. Depending on what teaching series other churches in the area were doing, I felt free to attend wherever I felt led. My goal had been to learn as much as I could wherever I could. I felt that part of my freedom was being taken away, but then I realized that God might want to use me in a deeper way.

Now that I had the time, I took a step of faith and decided to sign up for the membership classes. The decision brought me peace, joy, and a sense of belonging. It was time, and God had things for me to do.

Free to Serve

The Lord has things for all of us to do. In fact, we are called to serve one another. Jesus gave us the perfect model of serving when he washed the disciples' feet at Passover so many years ago. We are to serve not only our families but others in need. Serving helps us to look outside of ourselves and into the pain of someone else.

Although I had been attending Trinity regularly for several years and was faithful in tithing, I was not involved in any ministries or service capacity other than leading the Bible studies.

Lord, please show me where you would have me serve.

"Hey, Ariel," my friend said cheerfully one morning at church. "How would you like to be a greeter on Sunday mornings? I think you'd be great at it, since you're so friendly. You can try it for three months and see how you like it."

"That sounds like something I could do. I've been looking for a place to serve," I replied.

Wow, that was easy. All I had to do was ask God where He wanted me, and He answered.

Trusting Again

Responsibility, commitment, and service are things with which many of us struggle. Perhaps it is a fear of losing one's freedom, of submitting to authority, or of being taken advantage of that stems from painful events of our past. It was time to learn to trust again.

Joining the church was a big step of faith. It meant I no longer had the freedom to venture from church to church, because I had committed my time and services to one. In a way, this is similar to getting married. When we marry, we agree to forsake all others and commit our lives to loving and serving one person. In the same way I learned to surrender my time and schedule to serve at church, so, too, do married people learn to surrender themselves to serve their spouse, their family, and their community.

Be faithful in the small things God asks you to do, and He will allow you to do even greater things for Him.

It felt like I had taken a twenty-year detour into God's permissive will and had finally found the path back to God's perfect will for my life.

Few of us stay on the right path all our lives, but following God will always lead us in the right direction.

Step to Faith: Work through the tough trials and tribulations of life so that I may reap a harvest of peace and freedom.

And the God of all grace, who called you to his eternal glory in Christ, after you have suffered a little while, will himself restore you and make you strong, firm and steadfast. (1 Peter 5:10)

CHAPTER 16

Lighten Up

Don't we all want to be happy and full of joy? What do we need to do to achieve the happiness and joy we seek? What keeps us from feeling this way much of the time?

The United States Declaration of Independence says:

> We hold these truths to be self-evident, that <u>all men are created equal</u>, that they are endowed by their Creator with certain unalienable Rights: that among these are <u>Life, Liberty and the pursuit of happiness</u>.

What is happiness anyway? Many confuse happiness with joy. Both result in good feelings, so it is easy to see how they can be mistaken for one another, but are they the same thing?

Happiness is a state of contentment determined by our external circumstances and is temporary at best. We are happy when we are doing something fun, like dancing, playing a musical instrument, or being with good friends.

But happiness is fleeting. A phone call from a grouchy relative can ruin our mood in seconds, can't it? As our circumstances change, so does our degree of happiness. Now, I know that external factors can get to us at times, and that's normal to a degree. But what I am trying to suggest here is that we become more aware of the impact of these things so that we can combat them and have more happiness in our lives.

Do any of us want to walk around feeling gloomy for days on end because of the weather? Or the fact that our favorite sports team lost the game? Or even the sad fact that a loved one is not making wise choices? These things are out of our control, and one thing I've learned is that if I want to live a victorious and happy life, I cannot let things that are out of my control affect my state of mind.

Happiness is a Decision

Happiness is a decision I make every day when I wake up. Hanging in my office where I can see it every morning is a photo of a beautiful sunrise over a California beach I visited years ago. This scripture verse is written on it:

> *This is the day that the Lord has made. Let us rejoice and be glad in it.*
> (Psalms 118:24 ESV)

It is a reminder that I can make a conscious choice to be happy regardless of whatever circumstances I may find myself in that day. The Apostle Paul said, "I have learned the secret of being content," (Phillipians 4:12) and that is what I have learned to do as well. It is not always easy, but it is far better than wasting one precious day of my life being miserable. We will never live this day again.

Each day is a gift, and that is why it is called the present. Life is too short. None of us knows how long we have on this earth. Why waste a single moment being unhappy over things that someone said or did to us—basically because of other people?

Don't Take It Personally

It is a sad reality that people say and do things that hurt others, because they themselves are hurting. Much of the time it is not about us; it is about them. I used to get my feelings hurt so much, until I learned not to take things personally. It was a huge realization that freed me from a lot of angst, anxiety, and pain.

To maintain my happiness, I also learned to separate my sense of self-worth from what others say or do to me. People tend to take out their frustrations on those closest to them, and I needed to learn to deflect these hurtful comments rather than take them to heart. I didn't have to let their hurtful words and actions affect me so deeply. Detaching in love helped me to maintain my sense of well-being while still showing compassion for the pain of others.

Pay Attention

The only person I have control over is myself. I needed to learn to respect myself enough to put a stop to hurtful behaviors from others. But more important, I needed to learn to stop hurting myself by paying attention to what was going on inside.

We each have a voice that must be heard and listened to. Our feelings and emotions are speaking to us, and they try to get our attention by various behaviors and habits.

When we learn to listen to ourselves, we will be able to control our reactions and responses, as well as who and what we allow into our lives. Only then, we will be able to maintain not only our peace and joy but our self-respect as well.

Happiness is fleeting, but joy is everlasting.

What Is Joy?

Joy is an inner delight that pervades my soul despite my external circumstances. It fills me with an exuberance and zest for living. Joy comes from knowing I am in right standing with God and have positioned myself to share in the riches of Christ. Jesus lives inside me, and that's where joy resides as well.

Joy also comes from knowing that God is in control and that whatever comes into my life is because He allowed it and has a purpose for it. Yes, trials are tough, but we can still rejoice knowing that God is building our faith, character and endurance.

> *We can rejoice, too, when we run into problems and trials, for we know that they help us develop endurance. And endurance develops strength of character, and character strengthens our confident hope of salvation*
>
> (Romans 5: 3-4 NLT)

This frame of mind gives me strength to get through the potholes in life. Knowing that Jesus suffered infinitely more than I ever will gives me the courage to persevere.

An Attitude of Gratitude

Having joy does not depend on having everything we think we want nor having everything perfect in our lives. It is a choice we make to be thankful for what we already have. Being thankful and maintaining an attitude of gratitude are key components in remaining joyful.

> *Always be joyful. Never stop praying. Be thankful in all circumstances, for this is God's will for you who belong to Christ Jesus.* (1 Thess 5:16-18)

When times are tough it is easy to become disconnected from God. Trials can zap our energy and our zest for life. Despair and hopelessness can set in if we're not careful. As human beings, we tend to focus on our problems instead of God's promises. As spiritual beings, we know that God is faithful to bring us through the storms and that we are not alone. It is in the hurricanes of life that the time we have spent studying God's word really pays off.

> *"In this world you will have trouble. But take heart! I have overcome the world."* (John 16:33)

Joy must be guarded and protected. Are you frowning or smiling today? If I am not smiling, singing, and feeling carefree, these are signs that my joy has been depleted, and it is time to recharge and rejuvenate. There are several techniques that I have discovered over the years that help me to replenish my joy.

Maintaining Joy

I begin my day with a conscious decision to have a joyful perspective. When times were the most difficult, I repeated these two verses over and over till they became part of my everyday thinking.

> *The joy of the Lord is my strength.* (Nehemiah 8:10 NLT)

> *This is the day the Lord has made; let us rejoice and be glad in it.* (Ps. 118:24 NIV)

First, I start with the basics. I make sure I am well rested, eating healthfully, and getting my exercise. It is very easy to become discouraged if I am overly tired, haven't eaten properly, or haven't exercised my body. Taking care of my physical needs is the foundation. As Dr. Charles Stanley puts it remember the acronym "HALT." Never let yourself get too *H*ungry, *A*ngry, *L*onely, or *T*ired[1].

Second, I do something to clear my mind. It could be cleaning house, going for a run, or listening to some music. After clearing the mind, it is important to fill it with positive thoughts.

Third, and perhaps most important, I make time for regular periods of solitude. Solitude is crucial for connecting to ourselves and to God. The disciplines that I have developed over the years that have helped me to connect are reading sacred literature, journaling, prayer, and meditation. Whatever your spiritual path is, I encourage you to make these a priority. Spend time in meditation, prayer, and solitude. Give yourself the gift of quiet, so you can listen to what your heart and mind are saying to you.

I can't stress enough the importance of these activities. Steven Covey, author of the best-selling book *7 Habits of Highly Effective People*[2], calls these Quadrant 2 activities, which mean they are important but not urgent. They do not press upon us, but we must act on them. They are vital to achieving the kind of joyful life we want to have.

A Daily Process

Maintaining joy is a daily process and a mental and spiritual discipline. Just as we discipline ourselves to maintain our bodies and our health, in a similar way we can discipline our minds and spirits to maintain joy. Every day is a battle that begins in our minds and our thoughts. Unless we learn how to control our thoughts by prayer and meditation, we will never achieve victory in our lives. When I make the time to pray, I gain clarity on what's bothering me, and I see things from a different perspective. When I meditate, answers come, and my joy is restored.

Do the Right Thing

Joy is also a product of doing the right thing. By doing the right thing, I mean making wise choices. Making a wise choice means choosing today what you will be happy with tomorrow. Focus on the long term and the big picture. It is too easy to choose based on what feels good at the moment. We might be happy for a while, but there are two questions we need to ask ourselves. The first is, "Will I be happy with this choice in the long run?" The second is, "Will I be happy with the consequences of this choice?"

Sometimes, we have to suffer awhile doing the right thing in order to achieve a life of peace in the long run. But eventually, by continuing to make wise choices we will achieve a peaceful life and then be filled with joy. Joy comes from the realization that we have made good choices and are reaping the rewards of self-control and self-discipline.

Making decisions takes faith: faith that God is guiding us and giving us wisdom. When I don't know what to do or which way to turn, I lean on these two verses:

> *Trust in the Lord with all your heart and lean not on your own understanding.* (Prov. 3:5-6)

> *If any of you lack wisdom, let him ask of God, who gives to all liberally and without reproach, and it will be given to him. But let him ask in faith, with no doubting, for he who doubts is like a wave of the sea driven and tossed by the wind.* (James 1:5-6 ESV)

It will not always be easy. In fact, I have learned that most of the time, the right choice is often the most difficult. But God never allows us to go through things alone. He is always there if we reach out to him.

> *I will instruct you and teach you in the way you should go;*
> *I will counsel you with my eye upon you.* (Ps. 32:8 ESV)

Letting Go

There is one lesson that I keep having to learn over and over: the lesson of letting go. Joy cannot be achieved until we learn to let go. We learn the process of letting go in stages. We may need to learn to let go of material possessions, such as a 401(k), a job, or perhaps even a home. We also need to let go of negative thoughts and behaviors such as unforgiveness, fear, or anxiety.

Lastly, we learn to let go of people, pets, and places we have grown too attached to.

Letting go with love is important to building healthy, loving, and respectful relationships. I am guilty of taking on other people's responsibilities. The result is I get overstressed and worn-out. When I do for others what they could be doing for themselves, I steal the chance for them to feel good about themselves and their accomplishments. And I neglect my own responsibilities. I may feel like I am trying to help, but in reality, I am communicating a lack of trust in their abilities to get the job done. Learning to support rather than enable and to take care of myself first have been lifelong lessons.

Holding Too Tightly

Whenever I am holding onto something or someone too tightly, God steps in and says, "Let go." We are not to be too attached to anything or anyone. Why? Because when that person or thing is no longer in our lives, we will feel the pain of loss, and that means losing our joy. Many times, I have held on to people and things that were hurtful for far too long. If I could only have let go sooner, perhaps the pain would not have been so intense. Yes?

As a mother, my most recent lesson has been in letting go of my youngest son, who recently graduated from college and is now pursuing his own life and career. It is a bittersweet victory. Although I know I have done my job as a parent and, in particular, as a single parent, by giving my sons roots and wings, it is still difficult to let go of them. The best thing I can do for all of us is entrust them into the care of their loving Heavenly Father and pray that someday, we will all find a balance of unity and interdependence.

It is a big step to be sure. Fear of being alone can hold us back from letting go. But we do an injustice to ourselves and our children if we hold onto them and don't allow them to pursue their own lives and dreams. When afraid we will be alone, have faith in the Lord's promise that He will never leave or forsake us.

> *And be sure of this: I am with you always, even to the end of the age.*
> (Matthew 28:20 NLT)

This letting go business is a lesson we all must learn. To maintain our joy, it is important that we learn to look at these lessons from a brighter perspective. If we continue to hold onto a thought pattern, a person, or a relationship when it is no longer beneficial to us, we are only hurting ourselves. The question we must ask is, "Is this bearing fruit in my life?" If the answer is no, it is time to let go and learn new ways of thinking and relating.

When we learn to let go, we make space in our lives for something better: more peace of mind, more harmonious relationships, more time to reevaluate our lives. Letting go is an opportunity to trust God more. If I have the courage to let go of whatever it is I am holding onto so tightly, the Lord always has something better in store for me.

Step to Faith: Let Go and let God.

Give all your worries and cares to God, because He cares about you.
(1 Peter 5:7 NLT)

Lighten Up

Now I know that much of this has been a bit heavy to digest, kind of like a thick steak: takes a while to chew on, sits in your system for a while, but is good for you every now and then. So I'd like to share one more thing I've learned along my journey.

Many of you have already learned this one but I'm a slow learner. The thing is this: learn to lighten up. Life is heavy enough without us taking things so seriously all the time. Life is short. Enjoy the ride. Learn to see the humorous side of situations and use laughter when appropriate to lighten up tough conversations. When someone is "plucking your last nerve", as a good friend puts it, make a joke to ease the tension, but be sure the joke is not at his or her expense.

Laughter also keeps us young. As Victor Hugo, the French novelist and poet put it, "Laughter is the sun that drives winter from the human face."[4] If we try to see the humor in a situation, it might take some of the stress out of life.

It is also important to learn not to take ourselves too seriously. We are all human and we each have our own sensitivities. When

I realize I have hurt someone's feelings, I apologize quickly and sincerely. Saying those two little words "I'm sorry" can go a long way toward restoring harmony in the relationship.

Step to Faith: Learn to lighten up.

A cheerful heart is a good medicine, but a broken spirit saps a person's strength. (Proverbs 17:22 NLT)

CHAPTER 17

Live in Harmony

A good artist or musician knows what it means to play in harmony. The dictionary defines harmony as "a consistent, pleasing or orderly arrangement of parts; congruity"[1]. Harmony is also defined as "internal calm or tranquility"[2].

As it is pleasing to hear a harmonious melody, so is living in harmony. When we live by faith, we keep in rhythm with the orderly pace and flow of God's will for our lives.

The Chords of Harmony

The first chord to living a harmonious life is to find out if there really is a God. We all have our doubts at times, but let me reassure you – God is REAL!

Look at the beauty and wonder of nature, the order of the heavens, and the intricacy of the human body. There is an intelligence beyond our own that we can trust.

Ask Him to reveal himself to you and He will. As a father welcomes a prodigal son, so our Heavenly Father welcomes His children back with open arms ready to bless us beyond our wildest dreams. He is still waiting for us to come back and He always gives us another chance. We have nothing to be afraid of because God holds nothing against us. Will we keep coming back to Him?

The Second Chord

As one learns to sing in harmony by listening to the voices in the group, so too can we learn to live in harmony by listening to His Voice. At times, we all wonder whose voice to listen to, don't we? We wonder who God really is, what He thinks and what He wants us to do and say. But we don't have to wonder. We have the answer and it is this.

Jesus.

Look at what Jesus says and does, and then you will come to know His Voice. Jesus, like the famous soft drink, is the real thing: refreshing, invigorating, and completely satisfying. I encourage you to take a sip of the water of life and you will never thirst again.

He is a friend who will never abandon us, always accepts us, and who is always there to listen. Now, whenever you are ready, there is one final chord.

The Third Chord

The trials and tribulations of this world are ever increasing and to fight the battles of today as well as the future, we need more power. The Greek word for power is *dunamis,* from which the word dynamite comes from, which means strength, power, and ability.[3] When we accept Jesus into our hearts, we also receive the power of the Holy Spirit, our strongest ally. The Holy Spirit is with us to guide us, comfort us, and give us supernatural strength in times of need. He helps us overcome situations we cannot overcome with mere human strength. With these three chords, we can live a life of love, joy, and peace, but we need to do our part to stay in harmony.

Staying in Harmony

Three practices help us stay in harmony with God: praise, prayer, and meditation. Think of these as the songs we sing to God.

Praise is joyful adoration and acknowledgement of who God is and what He has done in my life. It is a celebration of the many mountains He has helped me to climb. Praise can be in many forms such as singing, playing music, and words of exaltation.

Someone once asked the question "Why should I praise God?" and the answer is: to acknowledge His sovereignty in our lives and to help us realize it is through Him that we live and move and breathe. Praise creates an atmosphere for God to release miracle blessings in our lives.

Prayer is the practice of communing with God. I like to think of prayer as speaking to God and meditation as listening to Him. Prayer opens the lines of communication. When we make time to share our hearts with God, we develop a more intimate relationship with Him. His phone line is never busy and He always picks up.

As in any good relationship, communication is a two-way street, and God wants to speak to us as well. The problem is we are usually too busy to listen. Meditation teaches us to slow down, quiet our minds, and still our thoughts so we can hear what He has to say. In time, we will hear His Voice throughout our day because we will have learned to tune out the distractions and noise that try to veer us off course.

I cannot emphasize enough the importance of praise, prayer, and meditation. Daily, consistent time together is as vital to developing a growing relationship with the Lord as it is with your best friend or spouse. I encourage you to make all three of these practices a daily part of your life and soon you, too, will have a vibrant love relationship with your Heavenly Father.

Dancing With God

Walking in faith is a beautiful dance with God. Although not all of us are dancers, I trust you will appreciate the analogy of the following poem written by an unknown source.

Dancing With God

When I meditated on the word *Guidance,* I kept seeing
"dance" at the end of the word. I remember reading that
doing God's will is a lot like dancing.
When two people try to lead, nothing feels right. The
movement doesn't flow with the music, and everything is
quite uncomfortable and jerky.
When one person realizes that, and lets the other lead,
both bodies begin to flow with the music.
One gives gentle cues, perhaps with a nudge to the back
or by pressing lightly in one direction or another.

It's as if two become one body, moving beautifully. The
dance takes surrender, willingness, and attentiveness from
one person and gentle guidance and skill from the other.
My eyes drew back to the word *Guidance*. When I saw "G"
I thought of God, followed by "u" and "i". "God," "u" and "i"
dance." God, you and I dance.
As I lowered my head, I became willing to trust that I would
get guidance about my life. Once again, I became willing
to let God lead.
My prayer for you today is that God's blessings and
mercies be upon you on this day and everyday.
May you abide in God as God abides in you.
Dance together with God, trusting God to lead and to
guide you through each season of your life.

You have turned my mourning into joyful dancing (Psalm 30:11 NLT)

Today is the Day

Now maybe you have read my story and you are still skeptical. Perhaps you have some fears, doubts or hurts that need time to heal. It's okay. God understands. He is waiting to embrace you with open arms and bless your socks off, but it is ultimately your choice.

God does not have favorites. What he has done for me He can and will do for you—if you are willing to trust Him. The adventure of your life can begin right now. Get rid of the baggage that's holding you back and be set free to embark on a journey of endless possibilities. You have nothing to lose and everything to gain.

What good is it if you gain the whole world, but lose your soul? (Mark 8:36 NLT)

Envision the life you dream of and then apply the simple steps described in this book. If we are willing to change our perspective and look through the lens of our spiritual glasses, we will begin to see miracles happen. When we activate our Faith, we open the channel for blessings to flow into our lives.

> *And without faith it is impossible to please God, because anyone who comes to him must believe that he exists and that he rewards those who earnestly seek him.* (Hebrews 11:6 NIV)

In this book, I have shared my most intimate and painful memories as well as some of my most joyful victories. My hope and prayer is that by seeing what the power of Faith has done in my life, you will be encouraged and inspired to activate it in yours.

I leave you with these famous words from Winston Churchill, "Never, never give up!" And until we meet, "Keep looking up!"

PRAYERS FOR MEDITATION AND RECITATION

The following are great prayers to use for daily meditation and recitation to strengthen your connection to God and to gain clarity, peace and wisdom. I encourage you to commit them to memory and they will serve you well.

This prayer is part of twelve-step programs such as Celebrate Recovery, Alcoholics Anonymous, and Al-Anon. The first few sentences may be familiar, but here it is in its entirety.

The Serenity Prayer

God, grant me the serenity
to accept the things I cannot change,
the courage to change the things I can,
and the wisdom to know the difference.
Living one day at a time,
Enjoying one moment at a time;
Accepting hardship as a pathway to peace;
Taking, as Jesus did, this sinful world as it is,
Not as I would have it; trusting that You will make all things right
If I surrender to your will;
So that I may be reasonably happy in this life
And supremely happy with You forever in the next.
Amen.

(Reinhold Niebuhr)

There are so many great prayers in the Bible. Here are three of my favorites:

We ask God to give you complete knowledge of his will and to give you spiritual wisdom and understanding. Then the way you live will always honor and please the Lord, and your lives will produce every kind of good fruit. All the while, you will grow as you learn to know God better and better. We also pray that you will be strengthened will all his glorious power so you will have all the endurance and patience you need. May you be filled with joy, always thanking the Father. (Col. 1:9–12 NLT)

Psalm 23

[1] The LORD is my shepherd, I lack nothing.
[2] He makes me lie down in green pastures,
he leads me beside quiet waters,
[3] he refreshes my soul.
He guides me along the right paths
for his name's sake.
[4] Even though I walk
through the darkest valley,
I will fear no evil, for you are with me;
your rod and your staff, they comfort me.

[5] You prepare a table before me
in the presence of my enemies.
You anoint my head with oil;
my cup overflows.
[6] Surely your goodness and love will follow me
all the days of my life,
and I will dwell in the house of the LORD
forever.

Psalm 37:1-10

[1] Do not fret because of those who are evil
or be envious of those who do wrong;
[2] for like the grass they will soon wither,
like green plants they will soon die away.

[3] Trust in the LORD and do good;
dwell in the land and enjoy safe pasture.
[4] Take delight in the LORD
and he will give you the desires of your heart.

[5] Commit your way to the LORD;
trust in him and he will do this:
[6] He will make your righteous reward shine like the dawn,
your vindication like the noonday sun.

[7] Be still before the LORD
and wait patiently for him;
do not fret when people succeed in their ways,
when they carry out their wicked schemes.

[8] Refrain from anger and turn from wrath;
do not fret—it leads only to evil.
[9] For those who are evil will be destroyed,
but those who hope in the LORD will inherit the land.

[10] A little while, and the wicked will be no more;
though you look for them, they will not be found.
[11] But the meek will inherit the land
and enjoy peace and prosperity.

APPENDIX A

Translations

Unless otherwise noted, scripture quotes are from the Todays' New International Version (TNIV): http://www.biblegateway.com

Other translations used are as follows:

New Living Translation (NLT)

English Standard Version (ESV)

New King James Version (NKJV)

King James Version (KJV)

Today's Living Bible (TLB)

APPENDIX B

Bibliography and Works Cited

Introduction

1. "faith." Merriam-Webster Online Dictionary. 2011.m.w.com Retrieved August 27, 2011 from http://www.merriam-webster.com/dictionary/faith

Chapter 4

1. "As the body without the spirit is dead, so faith without deeds is dead." James 2:26

Chapter 6

1. Jim Rohn, "Challenge to Succeed", CD program, 1991-2008. Jim Rohn International.

Chapter 11

1. Sugarland. "Settlin'." *Enjoy the Ride*. Mercury Records. 2006. CD.

Chapter 13

1. Albert Einstein, ThinkExist.com.Retrieved October 30, 2011 from http://ThinkExist.com/quotes/albert_einstein/

Chapter 15

1. Don Miguel Ruiz, *The Four Agreements*, (California, Amber-Allen Publishing,2007), 95.
2. Victor Frankl, *Man's Search for Meaning,* (United States, Beacon Press, 1959),104.

Chapter 16

1. Dr. Charles Stanley, Message entitled "Spiritual Shortsightedness", 1998.
2. Stephen R. Covey, *Seven Habits of Highly Effective People,* (Free Press, 1989)
3. Grant, Natalie. "Perfect People." *Relentless*. Curb Productions, Inc. 2008. CD.
4. Victor Hugo, Retrieved October 30,2011 from http://thinkexist.com/search/searchquotation.asp?search=laughter

Chapter 17

1. Retrieved November 5,2011 From http://dictionary.reference.com/browse/Harmony
2. Retrieved November 5,2011 from http://www.merriam-webster.com/dictionary/harmony
3. Retrieved October 30,2011 from http://www.truthnet.org/Holy-Spirit/5HolySpirit-Indwelling/Index.htm

AUTHOR BIO

Ariel Paz obtained her Masters Degree from Johns Hopkins University, speaks four languages, and has been an IT professional for over 30 years. She raised two sons as a single parent and hopes to be a grandmother one day. She fulfills her passion to encourage others through writing and blogging. Ariel enjoys dancing, tennis, soccer, travel, and loves to cook and entertain. She resides in Baltimore, Maryland and would love to hear from you.

Visit her blog, "Journey to Faith" at www.arielpaz8.blogspot.com. You can also follow her on Facebook, Twitter @ArielPaz08, and Pinterest.